# Spenser, Milton,
## and Renaissance Pastoral

9/28/81

# Spenser, Milton, and Renaissance Pastoral

## Richard Mallette

*Lewisburg*
*Bucknell University Press*
*London and Toronto: Associated University Presses*

© 1981 by Associated University Presses, Inc.


Associated University Presses, Inc.
4 Cornwall Drive
East Brunswick, New Jersey 08816

Associated University Presses
69 Fleet Street
London EC4Y 1EU, England

Associated University Presses
Toronto M5E 1A7, Canada

**Library of Congress Cataloging in Publication Data**
Mallette, Richard, 1949-
   Spenser, Milton, and Renaissance pastoral.

   Bibliography: p.
   Includes index.
   1. Pastoral poetry, English--History and criticism.
2. English poetry--Early modern, 1500-1700--History and
criticism.  3. Spenser, Edmund, 1552?-1599--Criticism
and interpretation.  4. Milton, John, 1608-1674--Criticism
and interpretation.  I. Title.
PR539.P3M3         821'.3'09145       78-73154
ISBN 0-8387-2412-4

*Printed in the United States of America*

To

**Helen Hanford Baldwin**

and

**Pearl Dahis Mallette**

# Contents

# Acknowledgments

Every student of Spenser and Milton knows only too acutely how deeply his indebtedness to the critics and scholars of the past couple of generations must extend. The variety and richness of the work which has illuminated the texts of these two poets can, of course, be a source of intimidation as well as inspiration and guidance. I have attempted to record, in the notes to the following pages, as much of my indebtedness (both inspiring and intimidating) as the vagaries of my memory have allowed. Students of the two poets and of pastoral literature will recognize other, unrecorded obligations and will, I trust, respond to them as signs of allegiance to the community of scholars.

My private indebtedness is more easily set down. For permission to reprint a somewhat revised version of chapter 2 my thanks go to *Studies in English Literature;* chapter 5 represents an expanded and revised version of an article published in *Modern Language Review.* I am grateful to Walter Kaiser, who read and reread the manuscript in various untidy stages. His good sense saved me from numerous blunders; his encouragement rescued me from much dismay. With characteristic generosity Judith Kates gave to two chapters her helpful attention. Matthew Gurewitsch brought his penetrating intelligence to a difficult stage of the argument; his scrutiny has made this book much clearer than it would otherwise have been. For advice in reading Virgil I join the ranks of those who are grateful to the late Reuben Brower. Both Neil Dugas and Claire Bergeron provided much needed material assistance. My greatest obligation is to the late Isabel MacCaffrey. Her own writing about Spenser and Milton has proved a constant source of ideas and direction. Her exacting standards of excellence and her advice at every stage of writing were offered with the magnanimity of a woman wholly devoted to the life of the mind. Finally, I must thank my parents, whose numerous kinds of support have made this and many other of my undertakings possible.

*She recaptured the sense of space, which is the basis of all earthy beauty, and starting from Howards End, she attempted to realize England. She failed—visions do not come when we try, although they may come through trying. But an unexpected love of the island awoke in her, connecting on this side with the joys of the flesh, on that with the inconceivable.*

—*E. M. Forster*

# Introduction

Literary history has associated Spenser and Milton, often rather loosely, if only because they wrote the two greatest heroic poems of the English Renaissance. While we seldom read their work in tandem in either the classroom or the library, we nonetheless acknowledge, perhaps glibly, that as children of the Renaissance Spenser and Milton share certain traditional values, beliefs, and ideas.[1] One of the best-known beliefs, accepted by these two poets more fervently than by any of their contemporaries, affirms that the noble aim of the poet is to deliver to the world an understanding of life in its fullest moral complexity, to breed, in Milton's words, "in a great people the seeds of virtue."[2] Spenser avers with equal assurance that the poet "thrusteth into the middest, euen where it most concerneth him, and there recoursing to the thinges forepaste, and diuining of thinges to come, maketh a pleasing Analysis of all."[3] Their immodest claims have not proved altogether unwarranted: we invoke a sobriquet such as the "poet's poet" or the "great blind bard" as a tribute to their success in portraying a world where chaos is man's lot and joy his highest expectation. We are always aware when we read Spenser and Milton that behind the fabric of the poem stands an all-seeing figure who, "teaching over the whole book of sanctity and virtue," promises that his vision can improve, even redeem our lives.

The pastoral poetry of Spenser and Milton never lies far off the course of the poet dedicated to the recovery of human perfection by means of his art. More than merely an exercise at an early stage of the poetic *scala*, situations and motifs of this ancient "kind" of verse figure significantly in their greatest poems. Spenser's devotion to the mode is self-evident: pastoral plays a role—often exclusive, sometimes peripheral, always self-assured—in nearly every poem he wrote, from *The Shepheardes Calender* to book 6 of *The Faerie Queene*. Milton, too, though characteristically suspicious of the frailties of the mode, even in the major poems never altogether abandons his own version of pastoral, as the opening line of *Paradise Regained* reminds us by categorizing *Paradise Lost* as a poem about "the happy Garden." In recent years we have increasingly recognized the prominence of pastoral in the work of both poets by exploring the bucolic "retreats" in the heroic poems, often by comparing their adaptations of this humble genre to their loftiest utterances.[4]

While testifying to the grip that pastoral exerted upon the imaginations of both men, the existence of Eden and the bowers and green worlds of Faerie tend to belie or undermine Renaissance precepts subordinating pastoral as a "lowly" genre, the hedge, as Sidney calls it, that poets "will soonest leap over."[5] Of course, it is a *topos* of pastoral literature that allows the poet-swain to voice his epic aspirations. But it hardly follows from there that the epic poet need regress to pastoral. Spenser's and Milton's persistent, even willful return to the fare consigned by contemporary dicta to poet-apprentices "at the first to trye ther habilities"[6] suggests they share a pointed and serious disposition toward pastoral, a genre that legions of their contemporaries indite as no more than "th' aboundance of an idle braine" (*Faerie Queene* bk. 2, Proem 1). This book will examine in detail poems in which Spenser and Milton fashion and animate a shared proclivity toward pastoral and will offer an account of this peculiar form of literary artifice from the perspective the poets have in common.

Virtually alone among the English Renaissance poets, Spenser and Milton develop in their pastorals profoundly self-conscious attitudes toward the poetic vocation and indeed toward the imaginative process itself. Recognizing an opportunity previously grasped fully by Virgil, both poets explore through the mode the complexity and conflicts of the poetic activity and ponder its value. The correspondences between Spenser and Milton to be discussed in this study indicate how both poets employ pastoral, often in quite different and unique ways, to understand, promote, and evaluate the enterprise of poetry. The pastoral poems presented in subsequent chapters focus on related aspects of lifelong preoccupations both poets share. How does the poet justify writing poetry in the large arena of life? If indeed he has been granted a special understanding of human experience, how is he to embody his vision in the difficult, often betraying medium of language? What is the relationship of poetry, and especially pastoral, with its palpable artifice and rigid formality, to the flux and disorder of life? The poet's powers, his failings, his aspirations, and responsibilities, as we find them repeatedly in the pastorals of Spenser and Milton, reveal a highly sophisticated poetics penetrating the recesses of their imaginative lives.

Because Spenser and Milton in their pastorals recurrently engage themselves as much with the inner life of the poet as with an ostensible "subject," a critical path through the relevant pastoral poems must concern itself with many of the patterns and dynamics, the signs and images of each poet's imagination. I say "relevant" because, of course, pastoral is a multifaceted genre, too broadly exploited and applied as a literary mode, even by Spenser and Milton, to conform to any single purpose or neat definition. Most conspicuously absent from the following pages are extended discussions of *Comus* or *Paradise Lost*. For all the affinities of these poems with Milton's other pastoral works, their pastoral emblems and themes do not explicitly serve the poet as a medium suitable to exploring the poet's vocation. While we may legitimately see the Miltonic poet in the figure of the epic bard or even in the Attendant Spirit, neither the narrative of the epic nor the drama of the masque offers a self-examining version of pastoral which elsewhere unites Milton with Spenser. Perhaps the magnitude of these two poems in Milton's canon has inhibited extensive critical scrutiny of the profound similarities between Milton's early poems and the Spenserian pastoral. A more exclusive concern with those poems where Milton and Spenser regard pastoral as a highly self-reflective form that anatomizes the poet's imagination does in fact illumine the total work of each poet. Accordingly, this study progresses from cardinal similarities between the poets toward their divergences. Such a sequence will establish, I trust, a firmer definition of each poet's imaginative orientation, while it casts on their pastorals a light intensive enough to distinguish their achievements from other practitioners'.

To many of those practitioners as well as to others in Spenser's and Milton's first audiences, neither *The Shepheardes Calender* nor the "Nativity" ode, both deeply indebted to the pastoral tradition, could have seemed at first glance an especially bold or unusual undertaking. E. K.'s public-relations work notwithstanding, each poetic debut dutifully observes the expectations of a readership accustomed to a young poet's conformity to the prescriptions of the poetic hierarchy. Spenser's verse prologue represents his eclogues as a "child whose parent is vnkent" and quickly makes way for E. K. to introduce the parent as a "yong bird . . . newly crept out of the nest," a novice "whose principals be scarce growen out." Milton, for whom such humility is unthinkable, nonetheless calls attention in his subtitle to the poet's juvenity. He wants to alert his audience to the fact that the poem he engendered in a direct line from Virgil's fourth *Eclogue* was delivered into the world on the eve of the precocious poet's majority.

Poet and audience alike looked emulously to Virgil's progress from pastoral tyro to epic bard; the Roman's unwitting imprimatur of the mode was further encouraged by schoolboy imitation of Mantuan's dour eclogues. In fact, eclogue writing served the Renaissance something of a salutary social function: Thomas Elyot maintains that the noble child, upon his initiation to Latin, ought to master Virgil's *Eclogues* in order one day to be a better governor.[7] Even as a principally literary enterprise, pastoral struck Sidney and Puttenham, as it did their Continental counterparts, as an excellent model for early emulation.[8] Low on the ladder of the poetic career, traditionally "base" in subject matter and "humble" in diction, pastoral exactly suited an age which cherished an unshakable conviction in the pedagogical and moral values of Art, Imitation, and Exercise. Requiring minimal narrative talent, even less experience of arms and politics, the form recommended itself to the poet unable or unwilling to challenge literary enterprises beyond his years.

But the history of the eclogue rewards us with recurring intimations of "greater things," the *maiora* (4. 1) of Virgil's Arcadian poet champing to exercise his burgeoning talents outside the pastoral arena. Thus, in the course of Spenser's and Milton's initiate poems, traditional gestures in deference to poetic decorum receive strong qualification, if not outright disavowal. E. K. calls upon us to witness "a diuine instinct and unnatural rage" in the course of his new poet's cycle of eclogues; the proem to Milton's ode foretells that the "sacred vein" of the poet's heavenly muse will join the angel choir to celebrate the Messiah's advent. Sanctioned by Virgil's precedent yet again, both poems immediately aim at realms higher than pastoral traditionally accommodates. The poet's crafty manipulation of decorum and tradition transcends the very genre he employs and inevitably draws our attention to his own prowess.

At the outset, then, we ought to acknowledge that notions of pastoral humility and decorum prove in practice to be part of a highly *recherché* activity. Often pastoral obeisance offered with one hand is taken back with the other; indeed it is flourished as a plume of the poet's sophistication, lest we forget that no small degree of talent and training precedes every memorable poem. After all, pastoral simplicity cannot be said to negate the Renaissance poet's ambition. More frequently, as Drayton expresses it, "the most High and most Noble Matters of the World may be shaddowed in [pastoral], and for certaine sometimes are."[9] In Spenser's and Milton's pastorals these noble matters frequently cannot be separate from the self-regarding world of the poet's imagination. In their initial endeavors, as in their pastoral poems repeatedly, we hear what seems to be the Olympian voice of the poet himself, directing our scrutiny to his wondrous skills, asking us to contemplate with him the vagaries of his imaginative life. Drayton's remark refers to the allegorical potentialities of pastoral he and his contemporaries exploit in order to glance at greater social matters. Spenser and Milton enrich their pastorals with the matters of the world as they interact with the matters of the poet's inner life. Their pastorals delicately figure forth the poet's aim, as Milton says, "to be an interpreter and relater of the best and sagest things" written by the "greatest and choicest wits of Athens, Rome, or modern Italy."[10]

# 1

## Spenser, Milton, and the Pastoral Tradition

*W*<sub>*hen*</sub> it came time to change his pastoral oaten reeds for the trumpets stern of epic, Spenser announced in his letter to Raleigh, "I haue followed all the antique Poets historicall." His eagerness to establish his sprawling poem squarely within literary tradition echoes a familiar humanist ideal whose English apogee we most often locate in Milton. The encyclopaedic imaginations of both poets are deeply implicated in literary retrospection. In fact, we readily associate Spenser and Milton partly because they pursued careers as richly diverse as their literary inheritance, making our image of each poet inseparable from his revered literary models. Their pastorals, no less than their heroic poems, embrace the Renaissance precept that in a poet's profound assimilation of the literature of his predecessors lies the opportunity to shape his contemporaries' future. "Following," as E.K. says, "the example of the best and most auncient Poetes, which deuised this kind of wryting," their pastorals are among the few that fulfill Ben Jonson's ideal of poetic imitation: "to draw forth out of the best, and choisest flowers, with the Bee, and turne all into Honey, worke it into one relish, and savour: make

19

our *Imitation* sweet: observe, how the best writers have imitated, and follow them."[1]

Because Spenser and Milton imitate the best writers so sweetly, we can easily misapprehend their choice of pastoral as a literary endeavor if we grant to the genre more than its due. "Whatever images it can supply are long ago exhausted," complains Dr. Johnson in one of his fiercer execrations of pastoral, and the modern reader of *England's Helicon*, to choose a ready specimen, would probably assent.[2] Perhaps pastoral notoriously eludes a satisfactory critical definition because its scant features resist sustained employment in a uniform and autonomous literary situation. As a result, pastoral more often is passively accommodated to other contexts than actively able to embrace a variety of expression or a wide range of experience. While the pliancy of the mode doubtless accounts for its endurance, the pastoral poet must pay a price not demanded by other major genres. He must choose to impose upon himself artifices (Johnson calls them "trifling fictions") of a severity and monotony characteristic of no other long-lasting mode. Etymologies of the terms "idyll" and "eclogue" remind us that restrictions are native to the genre. The poet may provide a "glimpse" in his idyll or make a brief "selection" in his eclogue, but in either case he imposes upon himself requisite limitations, both technical and psychological. Bound within a prescribed emotional range to a limited number of topics, the pastoral poet exploits *literary* experience much more thoroughly than, say, the satirist, or the epic poet, or the tragedian. The rustic poses, the stock *mise-en-scène*, the repeated formulas and situations that seem to find their way, with an almost liturgical persistence, into even the most sophisticated pastoral reflect the poet's obligation to rein in his energies under the bridle of inherited conventions.

But from a more positive and equally valid perspective, pastoral confinement often begets pastoral freedom. The fetters of literary convention paradoxically liberate the poet, as his mind, in Marvell's pregnant phase, "withdraws into its happiness." Within the boundaries of his literary circumscription the pastoral poet grants himself and his reader a refuge against the unlimited contingencies of fallen human experience. Excluding from his landscape the endless multiplicities of the day-to-day world, the pastoral poet rejoices in the sharply defined separateness of the pastoral environment,

> Annihilating all that's made
> To a green thought in a green shade.

Like the global epic poet, the pastoral poet requires a world of his own, a cleared space counterfeited from tradition and his own inventive wit. By emblazoning the hemmed enclosures of a green world distant from our own, the poet accentuates the finesse of his world-creating skills. Theocritus's famous description of the bowl in *Idyll* I, to which over forty lines are devoted, is the earliest example of the pastoral poet's desire to control and embellish his environment within circumscribed limits. In the very act of describing the scenes on the bowl's panels, which are entwined by an ivy frame, the poet obliquely renders a picture of pastoral life timelessly enshrined in the remote rural artifact.

The tendency to remove its activities as far as possible from the reader's daily world has been a distinguishing feature of pastoral from the beginning. Theocritus set his *Idylls* in remote Sicily, a location Virgil found uncomfortably close when he took up the shepherd's song. Virgil's decision to set his *Eclogues* farther afield, in Arcadia, and in doing so to replace the Theocritean open grove with the more sheltering and protective bower reflects the desire of the pastoral poet to seclude his poem from the everyday affairs of mankind.[3] Often his seclusion is temporal as well as spatial, for a retreat to a remote age when evil was unknown and nature sustained mankind in innocence and harmony lies at the heart of the pastoral vision.[4] "Pastoral is an image of what they call the Golden Age," says Pope in the preface to his own contribution to the genre.[5] He reminds us that the mythic roots of pastoral extend back to the genesis of mankind in the primeval paradise, that pastoral seclusion expresses the eternal attraction of primal perfection and the childhood of humanity.

The inherent literary retrospection of pastoral, then, cannot be segregated from the deeper longing for a vanished prelapsarian felicity. In his eccentric discussion of pastoral, Scaliger seems to have apprehended just such a connection, and then pursues it to a not wholly illogical extreme. The earliest herdsmen, this influential critic pronounces, produced the first pastoral poems, piping their idylls under the tutelage of the wind's rhythms and the bird's song.[6] Be that as it may, his hypothesis underscores how the pastoral poet's craving for the company of his literary forebears, for the roots of his art, cannot be dissociated from the general human longing for a mythic antiquity of harmony and pleasance. After all, Milton realizes Eden by means of specific literary echoes as evocative as our collective intuition that we once enjoyed such bliss. Even relatively undistinguished lines such as these from a poem in *England's Helicon* are meant to satisfy the reader by recalling a literary heritage as well as a vanished racial past:

> Hills with trees were richly dight,
> Vallies stor'd with *Vestaes* wealth:
> Both did harbour sweet delight,
> Nought was there to hinder health.
>     Thus did heaven grace the soyle:
>     Not deform'd with workmen's toile.[7]

The poet needs only the slightest detail ("richly dight . . . sweet delight . . . grace") when the verse achieves its effect by merely nudging the reader's mythic and literary recollection.

Virgil's first *Eclogue* offers a paradigm of the pastoral experience later poets emulate with varying degrees of success. The poet's astute insistence that we recognize the demarcation, however fragile, between the urban affairs of our fragmented world and the harmony of the *locus amoenus* demonstrates how the circumscriptions intrinsic to pastoral can be put to the service of pastoral freedom. Right at the start of his collection Virgil ironically grants his most extended and beautiful description of life in Arcadia to the dispossessed Meliboeus. Forced to accept his expulsion from the pastoral world by the encroachments of a voracious state and faced with a perilous future in our own world of history, Meliboeus speaks for all the dispossessed, all Virgil's readers who yearn to sustain with the landscape an intimacy that can never be fully prized until it is forever lost. Meliboeus's lament, which should be savored as one of the great statements of pastoral literature, marks the exclusion of the reader's previous notions of reality as he enters this distant Arcadian realm:

fortunate senex, hinc inter flumina nota
et fontes sacros frigus captablis opacum.
hinc tibi, quae semper, vicino ab limite saepes
Hyblaeis apibus florem depasta salicti
saepe levi somnum suadebit inire susurro;
hinc alta sub rupe canet frondator ad auras:
nec tamen interea raucae, tua cura, palumbes,
nec gemere aeria cessabit turtur ab ulmo.

[1. 51-58]

Happy old man. You will stay here between the rivers that you know so well, by springs that have their Nymphs, and find some cool spot beneath the trees. Time and again, as it has always done, the hedge there, leading from your neighbour's land, will have its willow blossom rifled by Hyblaen bees and coax you with a gentle humming through the gates of sleep. On the other side, at the foot of the high rock, you will have the vine-dresser singing to the breezes; while all the time your dear full-throated pigeons will be heard, and the turtle-dove high in the elm will never bring her cooing to an end.[8]

Every line of natural description after this point in the *Eclogues* is colored by the hopelessness that gives Meliboeus's lines their poignance. We belong with the exiled Meliboeus and may remain in Arcadia after his departure only by the grace of the poet who lets us in. This is why the poet never again matches, even in the astounding profusion of *Eclogue* 4, the sharply sketched, nostalgic picture in the first *Eclogue* of all that the dispossessed have lost. The shepherds who live in Arcadia are not of our party. "The rest of us," says Meliboeus, "are off—some to Africa, others to join the Britons, cut off from the rest of the world."[9]

Virgil's Arcadian poet, the avatar par excellence of Spenser's and Milton's pastoral spokesmen, presides over the *Eclogues* and serves as our guide and instructor in the collection.[10] Spanning the distance between Rome and Arcadia, he grants us our only access to the realm he depicts; we enter by his invitation and stay by his grace. Once inside, we range within the zodiac of his wit, responding to the inhabitants and situations there by means of his commentary. He assumes center stage in the opening of five of the *Eclogues* (2, 4, 6, 8, 10) and reminds us that his sensibility and craftsmanship confer vitality and meaning on the world he presents. His several addresses to Roman dignitaries remind us also that our imaginative journey to his green world has forced upon us a highly ambiguous perspective on the extra-aesthetic lives we must return to in the clay lodgings of the fallen world. But not until the last poem in the collection does the poet allow that harder world of history and geography actually to intrude upon Arcadia once again. At that point Gallus, a second representative of the dispossessed, enters the confines of the *locus amoenus*.[11] With him come the sleet of Macedonia and the tropic sun of Ethiopia (10. 66), inclemencies of a kind we readers know only too well. The final lines of the collection usher us out of Arcadia and leave behind its poet quietly weaving his mallow basket and singing serenely to the Pierides who sanctify his landscape.

Virgil's masterful realization of Arcadia sets forth in small compass the cardinal attractions of pastoral for Spenser and Milton. The comfort of withdrawing to a mythic and literary past entails another reward: we are always aware as we read the *Eclogues* that Arcadia is indistinguishable from the poem embodying it. The landscape, it inhabitants, and their activities exist and prosper, we sense, by virtue of the poet's ability to nourish and sustain them. Untroubled by responsibilities to verisimilitude, the poet never allows us to forget that Arcadia thrives thanks to his unique imaginative domestication. The chief fascination of the *Eclogues*, then, for poet and reader, lies in its patently literary quality. The *locus amoenus* is unchallengeably the *locus poeticus*.

To some extent I am describing pastoral, at least in its highly developed Virgilian form, as a prototype of fiction making. Such a claim is admittedly susceptible to aggrandizement and will eventually require qualification. But the pastoral poet's self-conscious fabrication of his rural artifice deserves recognition, especially in the light of Spenser's and Milton's highly self-conscious literary retrospection. In his cogent discussion of the Renaissance imagination Harry Berger describes the poetic act in terms that bear firmly on this aspect of pastoral. The "second world" of the imagination, Berger maintains, presents itself as a "model or construct which the mind creates, whose . . . essential quality is that it is an explicitly fictional, artificial, or hypothetical world. It presents itself to us as a game which, like all games, is to be taken with dead seriousness while it is going on. . . . Separating itself from the casual and confused region of everyday existence, it promises a clarified image of the world it replaces."[12]

This concept of the imaginative world, closely akin to

Sidney's Golden Nature, pertains not only to the pastoral environment but also to the identity of the poet as we find him in the pastoral poem. The distance between the "casual and confused region of everyday existence" and the transformed locality of the poem encourages—as the *Eclogues* powerfully attest—the separation of the historical poet and the poet-swain. With the accidents of everyday existence are altered the accidents of the poet's everyday identity. Such a transformation is intrinsic to the pastoral in ways that it may never have to be in, say, a love poem. The aesthetic distance of pastoral affords the poet and the audience the opportunity of stepping back to watch with some clarity the imagination at work. A consequence of this distancing can be seen in *Lycidas*. The effect of the double narrator, a device we are compelled to puzzle out as the focus retreats in the closing lines of the poem from the uncouth swain to the poet of the framework, lies at least partly in its shock value. The multiple perspective suddenly presented with the late introduction of this device forbids our easily assigning the "emotion" in the poem to any single sensibility. The intertangling roles of Milton, the poet, and the uncouth swain foster the disembodiment of the poem, so to speak. By the end of the poem we value it, in addition to the many other reasons one values *Lycidas*, for its objectivity, for its character as an artifact, an elaborately wrought object to be cherished for its workmanship.

Pastoral objectivity, then, has as much effect on the audience as on the poet. Because we, the audience, know that the green world to which we have been conveyed by the poet exists only by virtue of his skill as an artificer, we stand in a different relationship to the pastoral poem than we might to other kinds of poems. We stand farther away. "The bucolic dream," as Renato Poggioli says, "has no other reality than that of imagination and art."[13] The audience knows this and indeed derives pleasure from the contemplation of that distinct "reality." Even the most fleeting lyrics in *England's Helicon* can be valued more fully if the reader accepts their delightful objectivity and admires from a distance.

But a pleasure in the formal display of convention and in an exhibition of the poet's confecting skill, though essential to the mode, can be only the beginning of the serious poet's pastoral venture. For Spenser and Milton the reader can never be allowed merely to repose in admiration of the poet's skill as an artificer. How pastoral objectivity can be manipulated as an instrument of the dedicated poet's complex moral purposes can be illustrated by "Januarye."

For all its technical virtuosity, the eclogue that opens *The Shepheardes Calender* resembles in many ways less distinguished Elizabethan pastoral lyrics in its playful presentation of a love-sick swain. Later in the *Calender* we have to take Colin's hopeless infatuation more seriously, so that in retrospect this first eclogue is given depth by its position in the completed work. For the moment, though, we find ourselves amused by the studied posture of this forlorn lad, whom the narrator himself cannot help but drily mock: "May seeme he lovd, or els some care he tooke" (9).[14] The very presence of the narrator, who provides a framework to a poem that at first glance would seem more comfortable as a direct lyric, alerts us to the effort Spenser makes in "Januarye" to disengage his audience from the situation of its hero.

Colin Clout may be the hero of "Januarye," but the narrative poet of the framework wins our confidence and serves as our mediator. In his perceptive reading of the eclogue Hallett Smith has pointed out how Spenser achieves a kind of distancing effect by portraying "both shepherd and nature in perspective, in the round." By involving his reader only reservedly with the fortunes and feelings of Colin, Spenser succeeds in keeping his reader at arm's length from the emotion in the poem.[15] We may add that, while Colin is presented at a distance for our amusement and interest, the poet himself speaks to his audience as peers, up close, and thereby enlists our loyalty. The opening lines,

> A Shepeheards boye (no better doe him call)
> When Winters wastful spight was almost spent,
> All in a sunneshine day, as did befall,
> Led forth his flock, that had bene long ypent,

with the belittling parenthetical qualification, establish the poet's social ease with reference to his sophisticated audience. We are included in an elaborate game that gains further interest in later episodes of the *Calender* when our sympathies for Colin are gradually aroused by the startling depth of his feelings.

Although we enter "Januarye" through the gateway of the narrator's sensibility, we remain on the fringes of the scene that Colin presents. The narrator tells us that this is a "sunneshine day"; but the burden of Colin's lament rests on the hoary frost and "drery ysicles"(36) that he sees in his landscape. The bond between the shepherd and the landscape he addresses excludes both narrator and reader, who in turn are joined together by a peculiar social bond. Having crystallized the landscape and the shepherd within the confines of the scene, Spenser manages to deflect the center of interest from Colin and his landscape toward the stylizations and workings of the eclogue itself: "Well couth he tune his pipe, and frame his stile" (10).

Spenser's complex technique in this seemingly simple poem expertly fulfills the paradox of pastoral objectivity. The reader is engaged by the narrator and invited into the poem only to be kept disengaged from Colin and his song. The poet has amply flourished his talents by eliciting from his reader a multifaceted response. We cannot dissociate our heed of Colin's predicament from either the emotionally belabored landscape or the framework poet's highly colored presentation and commentary. The reader's continual sensitivity to the verbal dexterities so flamboyantly animating the entire artifice, then, unifies the poem and harmonizes its various features. We, the audience, participate in the imaginative act and are thereby enticed into a realm which would otherwise remain sealed off from our sensibilities. This is a reward seldom bestowed upon the reader of pastoral poems: imaginative participation of this quality is usually the province of the theater. Yet in the pastorals of Spenser and Milton the reader's participation is absolutely crucial; on its degree hang the fortunes of the poem.

A discernible pattern emerges when the pastoral poems of the two poets are placed cheek by jowl. The hero immediately presents himself to his readers either as their peer or as their gifted spokesman. Even though the setting of the pastoral poem is remote from the reader's everyday life, the tone he initially hears encourages a sympathetic response. In the opening lines of "Januarye" the poet speaks to us as his social peers and with no small degree of amusement invites us to attend to the plaints of an endearing, albeit naïve shepherd minstrel. We are drawn into the peculiar, remote landscape of the *Calender* and kept there by dint of tiny social acts such as these. E.K.'s scholarly paraphernalia serve a similar function: he invites us to contemplate these apparently simple eclogues from his own sophisticated level, from a perspective open not to the shepherds themselves but only to the educated urban readers. Throughout the *Calender* this method prevails. In "Aprill," for example, before we are ravished by the hymn to Eliza, we overhear a homely conversation between Hobbinol and Thenot about their friend Colin. The effect of the framework in the eclogue serves a number of purposes. The hymn itself is established as a feature of rural life, and moreover we can penetrate more deeply into the paradoxical nature of Colin himself, capable simultaneously of self-demeaning passion for Rosalind and ennobling praise of Eliza. The celebration of Eliza, then, where we are asked to participate in the poet's awesome vision, is made more accessible to our understanding by its context in the everyday chatter between two shepherds about their friend.

Thus are the monotony and limitations endemic to pastoral variegated and overcome in the hands of its greatest practitioners. While it is certainly true that the pastoral poet's verse—even in Spenser and Milton—does not resemble natural speech or attempt to surpass the inhibitions of the genre by imitating private colloquial utterance, at its most adroit the pastoral poem defines for us its unique purpose and identity. One of the more expert features of such a definition is the poet's creation of a pastoral hero, a feature notably absent in the common run of pastoral poems. After all, one hardly confuses Spenser's pastoral heroes with Milton's young spokesmen, or Colin Clout with Virgil's Arcadian poet. Each of these pastoral personae has distinct characteristics, in the sense, for example, that we can identify as a presence in the *Eclogues* Virgil's Arcadian poet, who resembles what we reckon to have been an accomplished and sophisticated young Roman poet. Or we can speak profitably about Milton's early personae as all working, however fitfully, toward an unshakable belief in the power of poetic truth to place human experience in the context of eternity.

This is the paradox Spenser and Milton relentlessly amplify in their pastorals: within the confines of a relatively rigid and apparently limiting set of literary conventions, whose effect would seem to hamper individual expression, the poet is capable of voicing his most individual concerns, of creating a highly personal mode of writing with a distinguishing voice and identity. Both poets endow their pastorals with engaging personae to whom we respond as characters. Colin Clout and Milton's poetic spokesmen present for our inspection complexities reflecting those of life. By endearing themselves to us as intriguing, often baffling personalities, characters such as Colin or the elegist of *Lycidas* sustain our enjoyment of the poems in which they figure. More significantly, their winning of our interest enhances the possibility of our grasping alongside them the great visionary moments to which their poems inexorably lead.

In *Lycidas* the reader's sympathies for the elegist are enticed from the beginning. Not only do we learn that he is weighed down with grief, but more important, we know that his grief is unwarranted by his youthfulness. His rude fingers ought not to be plucking the emblematic berries of sorrow, and certainly not for a contemporary. Throughout the first stage of the poem (1-85) the elegist dwells on details that emphasize his youth: his awareness of his "destin'd Urn"(20) is that of a young man contemplating his own death for the first time; his recollection of his idyllic childhood with Lycidas and his doubts concerning the homely slighted shepherd's trade awaken in the reader similar youthful responses to the anxieties of life. By first reliving with the elegist experiences common to all men at the beginning of maturity, the reader is prepared for the full impact of the later visions of the flowers, the sounding seas, and finally Lycidas mounted high.

Moreover, the reader's sympathies with the elegist are not won by sacrificing the deliberately distancing pastoral conventions in this, the most conventional great poem in the language. It is precisely Milton's exhaustive plundering of the resources of the pastoral elegy that eventually ensures our imaginative participation in the poem. We enter an environment so foreign to our own that we obey its laws and abide by its habits. Like other pastorals of Spenser and Milton, *Lycidas* achieves its effects by virtue of assuming at once an intimacy and a remoteness with respect to the reader. We attend to the elegist's well-being in the rarefied pastoral forum because we must enter a sphere so different from our own that we surrender to the imagination who guides us along its terrain. By means of the unique, often complex bond forged between the reader and the pastoral hero, Spenser and Milton at their most accomplished exploit the interplay between the public, literary aspect of pastoral and the private, intimate potentiality it paradoxically allows.

It is not unusual, given this paradox, to find in criticism the identification of Colin Clout with "Spenser," or Milton's personae with "Milton." Yet whatever the similarities between the speaker and the poet himself may be, it is dangerous to deny the distance between the two. In any literary work the author chooses a voice or voices with particular qualities that convey his attitude toward his subject and his audience and that can never be completely identified with the historical author himself. The choice of the shepherd's role, so palpably distinct from the actual circumstances of the poet's life, accentuates the feigned quality (in Sidney's sense) of the poet's choice. For example, while it may be convenient to think of L'Allegro and Il Penseroso as contrasting aspects of a personality we call "Milton," the very choices that the poet made in creating these speakers alert us to his detachment from them. Or, more important, unless we are willing to separate Spenser from Colin Clout, we can make little sense of the detached and often adversely critical attitude that the poet assumes, and wishes us to assume, toward the swain in *The Shepheardes Calender*. We are meant to follow his wasting over the year, as the seasons take their toll and his face grows furrowed, from a perspective similiar to Spenser's own—kindly, but distant.

The balanced perspective poet and reader share bears on many features of Spenser's and Milton's pastorals, not least of which is the role of the landscape. Spenser's and Milton's pastorals present the landscape much as Virgil presents his landscape: it stands as an extended figure of the poet's imagination, or, as Bruno Snell says of Arcadia, "a spiritual landscape."[16] Since the landscape embodies his inner life and provides an idyll of his creative faculty, the poet assumes varying and often conflicting attitudes toward it. In "Januarye" the landscape does not elicit a response from

Colin; rather, Colin summons from the landscape a response to his unhappiness. He addresses the landscape not in order to learn from its processes and secrets something about himself, but to give expression to what he already feels. The formal organization of the landscape as Colin presents it (i.e., creates it) actually becomes the formal organization of his song. Each stanza, as it presents a different facet of the natural scene, presents also a different facet of the singer's grief. The intimacy of the landscape with the pastoral poet's art forms the basis not only of the pathetic fallacy, but also of the more grandiose convention that leaves the landscape wild or dead in the shepherd poet's absence. In "Januarye" this intimacy is given a characteristic added dimension by the presence of the detached narrator. His separation from Colin's landscape symbolizes the poet's disengagement from his poem. We shall see that this poetic disengagement makes possible the great visionary moments that occur in Spenser's and Milton's pastoral poems when the physical limitations of the landscape are transcended.

These observations do not generally hold true for the non-pastoral landscapes that we find in Renaissance poetry, and the contrast helps to delineate pastoral more clearly. In countless lyrics, songs, and all through the miscellanies of the period, we find the poet turning to the natural processes of nature in search of a new understanding of himself and human experience. In the trees, the rivers, the hills and vales, the poet seeks out an analogue, whether in sympathy or in sharp ironic rebuttal, to his feelings. The main assumption, especially in the sixteenth-century lyric, is that the landscape provides a physical manifestation of a cosmic norm and serves as an image of the way life ought to be lived. In the appropriately titled "Melancholy," Thomas Lodge demonstrates this relationship clearly:

The earth, late choked with showers,
Is now arrayed in green;

Her bosom springs with flowers,
The air dissolves her teen:
The heavens laugh at her glory,
Yet I bide sad and sorry.[17]

The scene here—as opposed to those we find in Spenser and Milton—has something implicit to teach the poet. Even though his melancholy is accentuated by the freshness and profusion of the landscape, behind that contrast lies the conclusion that the poet's feelings are unbalanced and unnatural. Surrey's famous sonnet, "The soote season . . .," works by way of a similar contrast: the earth and its creatures, having renewed their lives according to seasonal rotation, highlight the poet's own sense of deviance:

And thus I see among these pleasant things
Each care decays and yet my sorrow springs.

Of course, this point can be exaggerated. The pastoral landscape, like its nonpastoral counterpart, offers a tonic for the unbalanced life that fallen man inevitably leads. This consideration lies at the heart of the pastoral vision and motivates, for example, the retreat of Rosalind and Orlando to Arden, where they are liberated and revitalized in ways forbidden by the corruptions of the court.

On the other hand, the landscape in Spenser's and Milton's pastorals receives different emphases from those visible in the general run of Renaissance poems that feature "natural" detail, including the pastorals of their contemporaries. The emphasis in Spenser and Milton is not on nature's teaching man, but quite the reverse, on the poet's leading, harmonizing, even "creating" nature. Like the skill of Orpheus, whose revered incarnation in Spenser and Milton makes him the patron saint of their pastorals, the poet's song gives to the landscape its well-being and order. This lofty claim is especially visible in its extreme forms, as in the assertion on the part of Colin Clout's friends that during his absence "all dead in dole did lie," but that

> . . . now both woods and fields, and floods reviue,
> Sith thou art come, their cause of meriment,
> That vs late dead, hast made againe aliue.
>
> [*Colin Clout*, 22-30]

Moreover, it holds true in less readily obvious ways; for example, the Miltonic poet, without overtly claiming his orphic gift, almost always demonstrates his control over the landscape by means of the control he exercises over its presentation. In *L'Allegro* the poet implicitly attributes the felicitous organization of his landscape to his own powers of perception:

> Streit mine eye hath caught new pleasures
> Whilst the Lantskip round it measures . . .
> Meadows trim with Daisies pide,
> Shallow Brooks, and Rivers wide.
> Towers, and Battlements it sees
> Boosom'd high in tufted Trees . . .
>
> [69-78]

Rather than depicting a landscape that exists independent of its observers, the speaker carefully arranges the details of his environment so that we learn a great deal about his sensibility from his measuring capabilities. In effect, he has captured and thereby "created" the landscape confining him. As "Januarye" in its quite different fashion also suggests, the poet in Spenser's and Milton's pastorals implicitly asserts his authority by continually reminding us that the verbal act is indeed the animus of the landscape.

The assertion of the poet's authority over his landscape and his poem also provides him the means of transcending the limitations of pastoral. Pastoral confinement allows the poet scale, hence progress from low to high. Virgil's portrait of Silenus in Eclogue 6 (18-26) is a graphic case in point. The dissolute old storyteller must be captured forcibly by his listeners and tied with his own poetic garlands before he will raise his voice to orphic pitch. In the same way, the elegist of *Epitaphium Damonis* must finally focus his attention on the rustic cups of Manso before his grief-ridden mind can ascend to the heavenly vision. The contrary dynamics of constriction and flight call for extended discussion in later chapters, but a few other examples can be prefigured now. Colin Clout must learn to "brydle" his passions before he can "mount as high, and sing as soote as Swanne" ("October," 90). Only after he has returned from his wanderings and is safe amidst an encircling company of friends, in *Colin Clouts Come Home Againe*, does he finally succeed in singing vatic truth. So, too, *Lycidas* initially presents a speaker unprepared and undisciplined, whose rude fingers are forced to attempt a task seemingly beyond their power. Compelled by bitter constraint, however, the elegist builds a lofty rhyme that gradually lifts him to an apotheotic vision. The speaker's emotional struggle to escape his initial confining grief greatly enhances the impact of his ultimate joy.

As varied as these examples are, they further delineate how Spenser's and Milton's pastorals exploit the conflict between the inhibiting restrictions of pastoral and the responsible poet's yearning to enunciate, in Ben Jonson's term, "something like Truth." While this conflict applies to almost any traditional kind of poetry, it has a special application here. In pastorals of Spenser and Milton the artifice of the conventions, always threatening to verge into triviality, confronts the soaring aspirations of a greatly gifted mind. Their exploration of this conflict often yields the profoundest rewards. For example, most poets gather their eclogues in a collection so as to impose variety where it would not otherwise exist. Spenser styles his collection of eclogues according to the seasonal cycle, under the pressure of which we witness at once Colin's debilitation and the joyous celebration of Eliza in the renewal of spring. Serious issues arise about man's life as a natural creature. On a less philosophical plane, in the *Epitaphium* Milton deploys the overused convention of the pastoral poet's sketch of his epic plans as an organic feature of his lament. As the elegist gropes toward a consolatory vision, he promises to fulfill his friendship with Damon by casting off the homely shepherd's cloak and mounting the epic steed to sing the glories of the English people (161-78). His elaboration of his epic plans does not merely release him from the confinements of his genre; he is simultaneously loosened from the bonds of his grief.

The poet in Spenser's and Milton's pastorals must transcend his genre and the landscape it embodies, just as he must transcend the fallen imagination which generates his pastorals. But the poet is tied to the sensory world of nature—whatever makes the too much loved earth more lovely—just as he is tied to his fallen imagination. The difficult ascent to perfection, as every neoplatonist knows, is achieved only by means of imperfect copies. By capturing, recreating, giving life to the landscape, the imagination can achieve a vision beyond nature. It can, however fleetingly—on Mount Acidale or at the end of *Lycidas*—glimpse the dancing Graces or fly beyond the sounding seas to the other groves and streams of the heavenly landscape.

The tension between the poet's soaring imagination and the restricting demands of his poetic form, a tension that vibrates from the core of Spenser's and Milton's imaginative lives, can be seen to fulfill the Renaissance understanding of the nature of poetry and the poet. When in *The Advancement of Learning* Bacon defines poetry as "a part of Learning in measure of words for the most part restrained, but in all other points extremely licensed and doth truly referre to the imagination, which [is] not tyed to the Lawes of Matter," he employs the same dichotomy between "constriction" and "flight" that we find in the pastoral poems of Spenser and Milton.[18] It is worth pursuing this opposition a bit further, especially as we find it in the familiar Renaissance belief in the poet as both "maker" and *vates*. For in trying to come to terms with the elusive nature of artistic creation, the theorists of the day posit two seemingly contradictory roles for the poet. These are expressed in terms strikingly similar to the images that animate the pastoral poems of Spenser and Milton. On the one hand, as everyone agrees, the poet is *vates*, a prophet possessed by poetical rapture, which, in Jonson's words, "riseth higher as by a devine Instinct . . . gets aloft and flies away with his Ryder."[19] Jonson insists that the two roles the poet plays are necessary to one another: the poet through proper discipline and imitation of the ancients learns to "ascend" to the highest reaches of *furor poeticus*. And in his own vivid way Sidney strikes a similar balance when he says that "the fertilest ground must be manured, the highest-flying wit must have his Daedalus."[20] It is worth noting, incidentally, that a parallel tension is embodied in Puttenham's oft-quoted observation that the purpose of pastoral is to allow the poet "vnder the vaile of homely persons and in rude speeches to insinuate and glaunce at greater matters."[21]

Having defined the poet's nature, Renaissance writers attempt also to define the nature of poetry and its value as a human endeavor. In this line of inquiry we may see fulfilled the retrospective movement that pastoral presupposes. When Milton in "Of Education" claims that the "end then of learning is to repair the ruins of our first parents by regaining to know God aright," he is voicing a familiar argument for the value of poetry, that he elsewhere claims "of power beside the office of a pulpit" to lead man toward regeneration.[22] The craftsmanlike poet, rigorously trained in the workshops of language and life, makes things that never were, or at least never have been since the Fall. As Bacon puts it:

A sound argument may be drawn from Poesy, to show that there is agreeable to the spirit of man a more ample greatness, a more perfect order, and a more beautiful variety than it can anywhere (since the Fall) find in nature.[23]

While Bacon's parenthetical "(since the Fall)" may seem off-hand, he refers to the precondition of all Renaissance poetic theory. Poetry, in delighting men to do good, "figures forth," in Puttenham's happy phrase, "the best, most comely and beautiful images or appearances to the soul."[24] The importance of the imagination resides in its ability to leap the distance between life as we know it and a life distinct and fully realized, unknown, as Sidney says, since "that first accursed fall of Adam."[25]

The retrospective attitude that the Renaissance deemed indispensable to a serious poetic vocation and, as I have argued, indispensable to pastoral, of course tells only half the story. No commitment to the didactic importance of literature could possibly exclude from its considerations a future orientation. The Horatian formula, *aut prodesse . . . aut delectare*, which the Renaissance found so agreeable and useful, justifies literature according to the benefits which the reader will reap. His life will be improved by the delightful teaching he assimilates from the poet's portrayal of "what may be and should be."[26] It is not surprising, then, when we consider how fully the pastoral poems of Spenser and Milton embody the values and hopes of the poet himself, to find how unswervingly their pastorals move from an initial retrospective attitude toward a concluding prospective utterance. By the end of their pastorals the constrictions of the movement to the past have been broken, giving way to a prospective vista characterized by images of flight and release. As we have seen, this release of energy often involves the poet in a consideration or an announcement of the greater things to follow in his career, a virtual obsession of Virgil's Arcadian poet. But at their most effective, Spenser's and Milton's pastorals widen their visions to encompass not merely the poet's own career, but also other aspects of life on which the poet's art bears. The poet of the "Nativity" ode, without finally allowing us to neglect the magnitude of his poetic feat, envisions on behalf of all humanity the day when "at last our bliss/ Full and perfet is" (165-66). Book 6 of *The Faerie Queene* provides perhaps the most satisfying example, because Spenser expertly aligns an often dangerous self-preoccupation to his theme, a new understanding of courtesy. The proem to the book finds the poet harking back to "Plaine Antiquitie," when courtesy and virtue flourished in human life. His nostalgia is not fulfilled until the narrative shifts to the green world in the climactic pastoral cantos. In this environment courtesy and virtue exist, at least briefly, uncontaminated by civilized life. So, in fact, does poetry. Colin Clout's poetic evocation of the vision on Mount Acidale inspires in the poet-narrator who witnesses it nothing short of *furor poeticus* (6. 10. 28). In his triumphant address to the Queen, who embodies courtesy at its most sublime, the poet renews his commitment to the promotion of virtue and prophesies its flourishing in "future age."

Virgil develops the progression from past to future that gives life to the dynamics of "constriction" and "flight" with instructive elegance. In his sixth *Eclogue* many of the patterns and themes Spenser and Milton rely on and refashion are given full expression. It represents Virgil's most explicit commentary on the pastoral mode and on the career of the pastoral poet. The poem embraces a temporal span from the distant and mythic past to the exalted future of the Arcadian poet himself, and much of the power that the poem achieves can be attributed to the interplay of the mythic quality of the narrative fable and the personal concerns of the poet.

The fable recounts the story of Silenus, the Dionysian singer of the world's origins, and, as Joseph Addison says, of the "most surprising transformations which have happen'd in Nature since her birth."[27] Preceding the fable is the poet's invocation, wherein he recalls his earliest verse, indebted to the Theocritean model, and other details of his personal chronology as it corresponds to the progression of the poetic hierarchy. Discouraged by Apollo's fiat from his exalted but premature ambition to rehearse tales of kings and battles and commanded to sustain his lowly bucolic role, the poet has humbled himself to the dictates of decorum (*non iniussa cano*, 9). But he finds consolation in the notion that the woods, after all, will resound with the name of Varus, the consul to whom the poem is dedicated. Satisfied with the glory that a dedication to such a patron will bring him in the eyes of Apollo, the poet proceeds zestfully to his fable. Already, then, within the confines of the introduction, we are provided with a temporal movement from past to future in terms of the poet's career, wherein he recalls his first happy attempt at imitating the distant originals of his genre and anticipates the satisfactions of later renown.

The narrative progresses according to a similar pattern. It too is the story of a singer called upon to perform; but in Silenus's case the swains of the countryside, and not Apollo, instigate the performance. Silenus's song, moreover, clearly outstrips in its effect any song within the Arcadian poet's capabilities:

> tum vero in numerum Faunosque ferasque videres
> ludere, tum rigidas motare cacumina quercus;
> nec tantum Phoebo gaudet Parnasia rupes,
> nec tantum Rhodope miratur et Ismarus Orphea.
> [27-30]

And now a miracle—you might have seen the Fauns and the wild creatures dance lightly to the tune and stubborn oak trees wave their heads. Rocky Parnassus is not so deeply moved by the music of Apollo; Ismarus and Rhodope have never known such ecstasy when Orpheus sang.

Neither Apollo nor Orpheus can match Silenus's power; we quite justifiably recognize in his ecstatic harmonies the highest, though unattainable, goal of the Arcadian poet's own aspirations. In fact, Silenus's narration of world history—the reign of Saturn, the tragedy of Prometheus, the madness of Pasiphaë—coincides with and may represent the fulfillment of the Arcadian poet's own ambition to narrate great feats.[28] Given the parallel between the framework and the fable, then, we expect the conclusion of the poem to look forward to the future. Silenus's last tale recounts the poetic inauguration of Gallus. Handed the reedpipe of pastoral song by Linus, *haec illi divino carmine pastor* (67), Gallus is instructed to sing the tale of the Grynean Wood and thereby to hallow it in Apollo's eyes. The poem concludes with the suggestion that Gallus does indeed fulfill Linus's imperative, but the poet himself is unwilling to pursue Gallus's career in detail (*Quid loquar*, 74). Because Gallus's success is only sketched, the poem ends on a deliberately inconclusive note. The open-ended quality of the closing lines reinforces the suggestion that the Arcadian poet's own ambitions have received vicarious fulfillment in the promise of Gallus's success as a sacred poet.

The important point here is that Virgil is playing a game. The Arcadian poet's fulfillment is not of course vicarious: he has fashioned his poem to its completion and incorporated within its boundaries realms of experience surpassing his humble expectations. By conforming to the requirements of pastoral decorum, he has suggested their transcendence. He has proved himself capable of generating not only an impressive series of mythological incidents but also surrogate poets to narrate them. Without making any overt claims for his own powers, he has nonetheless succeeded in portraying the conditions under which orphism is possible. That portrayal itself represents his own reenactment of the primal orphic rite, the taming of his own Arcadia, and his success as an artist.

The subtle pastoral poetics of *Eclogue* 6 takes us in some measure into the sensibility of the poem's creator. Even by itself, detached from the collection which it illuminates, the poem encompasses more than a mere preoccupation with poetic ambition: it surpasses the restrictions of pastoral and anticipates epic. The desire to write epic poetry is certainly a natural and legitimate concern of the pastoral poet, but it cannot be his only concern. An overwhelming and ultimately limiting preoccupation with the poetic vocation per se proves to be, in fact, one of the precipices over which Virgil's pastoral successors in the Renaissance repeatedly plunge headlong. It is no coincidence that the poem most frequently emulated by Spenser's "followers"—Drayton, Browne, Wither, Giles, and Phineas Fletcher—is "October." The subject of the poet's lot in life proves irresistible to a coterie that looks back fondly to the golden days of the Elizabethans, when poetry flourished and life seemed somehow better. While all too frequently we find in the Spenserians an exposed self-indulgence, a recurring note of self-congratulation, in Drayton, the most accomplished of the lot, we may view less distorted reflections of the pastoral achievements of Spenser and Milton.

Over his long career Drayton wrote and rewrote his collections of eclogues, and each edition reveals an increased interest in the poet's profession as a subject for verse. But as his confidence in the efficacy and influence of his profession diminishes over the years, his use of pastoral as a means of lamenting the decline of poetry and its debased social conditions increases:

The Groves, the Mountaynes, the pleasant Heath,
That wonted were with Roundelayes to ring,
Are blasted now with the cold Northerne breath,
That not a Shepheard takes delight to sing.[29]

The identification between poet and shepherd in Drayton, as in his confreres, is strong and uncomplicated; the poet's autobiography and pastoral situations seem often easily to correspond. The poet frequently employs pastoral as an elegant disguise to present his professional problems before the public, an undertaking with which the Spenserians, in Joan Grundy's words, "out-Spenser Spenser": "Above all [pastoral] provides the poet with a mirror in which he may contemplate his own image, as a poet. . . . The Spenserians exploit these opportunities to the full. Their pastorals are, predominantly, poems about poetry."[30]

This cannot be said—at least in the same way—about Spenser and Milton. One reason lies in their shared attitude toward their art. For Drayton and his confederates, poetry is a profession; for Spenser and Milton, poetry is a vocation. From the Spenserians we learn about the state of letters in their era; from Spenser and Milton we learn how the poet engages our sensibilities to create patterns of reality pertinent to the shifting fortunes of our own lives. Of course, like their less distinguished contemporaries, their pastorals are "about" poetry. But they are not only about poetry nor about poetry as a merely belle-lettristic enterprise. When the pastorals of Spenser and Milton draw us into their fictions in pursuit of the poet-hero, we attend with equal fervor the designs of our lives which the poet's art illumines. The special artifice of their pastorals, at once distant and intimate, engages poet and reader in a landscape of the imagination. For Spenser and Milton pastoral is more than a mode of self-contemplation: their pastorals bear witness to all human aspirations toward imaginative fulfillment. The poems on which subsequent chapters focus achieve their various effects by exploiting the interplay between the public realm and private sensibility, between distant past and hopeful future, between nature and art. They chronicle what happens when the poet steps before us, how the mission of the responsible poet is given life in his verse.

# 2

## The Shepheardes Calender and Colin Clouts Come Home Againe

$S$*penser's* longtime awareness of his historical, social, and literary responsibility "true vertue to aduance" (*Faerie Queene*, 5. 3. 3) receives unique expression in his two major pastoral poems. Perhaps because they were published at almost opposite ends of the poet's career, *The Shepheardes Calender* (1579) and *Colin Clouts Come Home Againe* (1595) have rarely suggested to critics that they share anything more extensive than their pastoral settings and their widely dissimilar versions of Spenser's "poetic spokesman," Colin Clout.[1] The *Calender*, of course, has enjoyed greater fame, because it marks both the debut of the professional English poet and a watershed in the development of native verse technique. *Colin Clout*, though, is the poem people usually enjoy more.[2] Doctor Johnson's complaint about the "studied barbarity" of the *Calender*'s diction or C. S. Lewis's objection that the eclogues are "rather dull" simply cannot be voiced against *Colin Clout*, where we have a fluent narrative, visibly unified, obviously the work of a mature, accomplished poet.[3] I find that the two poems are, or at least suggest, more nearly a single imaginative structure, and that, taken together, they comprise a diptych, a contiguous, self-conscious portrait of the Spenserian artist. In the picture of Colin Clout that emerges when the two pastorals are placed in the same perspective, we find that the "personality" of the earlier Colin complements that of his later namesake, that the two figures are as closely related in many ways as L'Allegro and Il Penseroso.

At the outset, a disclaimer is in order: I am not suggesting that Spenser consciously composed *Colin Clout* as a direct postscript or response to the poem that launched his poetic carer. Nor do I suggest that he wrote either poem as an anachronistic "Growth of a Poet's Mind." But his choice of Colin as the principal character in both poems, the numerous references in the later poem to the *Calender*, and the satisfying resolution in *Colin Clout* of Colin's earlier frustrated passion for Rosalind suggest that Spenser surely conceived of the two poems as somehow akin. Their kinship springs from the impulse of the imagination that Spenser shares with Milton: to find in pastoral a natural fiction able with all seriousness to explore the comprehensiveness of the poetic vocation. These poems, therefore, give expression to some of the practical problems that Spenser must have confronted in his own life. How does the poet employ his gifts and define his role in the drama of life? How does he reconcile his vaulting imagination to the demands of the world and the flesh, so precarious, so corruptible, so compelling? How, with his vision beclouded by unavoidable weakness and infirmity, does he attain a glimpse of truth that he can share with his fellowman?

My allusion to Milton's twin poems is useful in defining the structure that results when the *Calender* and *Colin Clout* are read in sequence. At first glance, Colin seems as different in each poem, as opposite in temperament as Milton's cheerful man from the pensive man. The *Calender* presents Colin primarily as a pathetic, even a tragic figure, whose destructive passion for the elusive Rosalind has isolated him from his peers and, even worse, by the end of the poem has ossified his obviously formidable poetic talent into woebegone speechlessness.[4] The Colin Clout who occupies our attention in the later poem, though, is of quite another stamp. He plays his self-appointed roles as social arbiter, didact, and mythmaker with all the aplomb and "wondrous skill" (897) of Orpheus himself.

But the differences that seem to separate the earlier Colin from his later namesake in fact accentuate the bonds that unite them. In the moments in the *Calender* when Colin overcomes his demeaning obsession with Rosalind in favor of ennobling praise of Eliza in "Aprill" and of Dido in "November," he clearly anticipates his later avatar. Early intimation of Colin's "aspyring wit," his unrealized power to "mount as high and sing as soote as Swanne" ("October," 83, 90), are strong enough to make his later performance the natural and decorous outcome of his once dormant potentiality. Just as in *L'Allegro-Il Penseroso*, the two portraits form a composite, in which the earlier figure matures gracefully into the riper, self-assured hero of the later poem. For all the diverse subjects and situations encompassed within both of Colin's poems, a central concern (again, much as in Milton's diptych) runs through both, in a pattern something like the neoplatonic ladder that Spenser often finds imaginatively attractive. We see this pattern almost visually in the pervasively vertical imagery, which at times, especially in *Colin Clout*, can be almost dizzyingly "aspyring." The imagery is appropriate to the vertical structure of the two poems taken together; it also reflects the course of Colin's personal progress as poet-lover, his long, arduous struggle to the top of the neoplatonic *scala*.

Spenser's commingling of neoplatonism and pastoral is one of the happiest and most appropriate unions. In the neoplatonic discussions and commonplaces of the day he found a great deal about both love and poetry, the predominant subjects of pastoral from Theocritus on. Exactly which

neoplatonic writers Spenser read or when he read them need
not concern us here.[5] As Robert Ellrodt points out, the notions of Italian neoplatonism were rife in England at the time,
and Spenser would have imbibed its commonplaces "from
the very air around him."[6] Doubtless, though, from his Cambridge days on, he was familiar with Thomas Hoby's splendid translation of *Il Cortegiano* (1561), where he could
discover the thorny ideas of Ficino in lucid, dramatic prose.
It is useful, then, as a prelude to ampler discussion of the
poems, to keep in mind the ways in which Bembo's theory of
love in the fourth book of *The Courtier* anticipates Colin's
progress as a lover-poet.

Bembo's discourse vividly outlines a personal regimen, intended to lead the individual or "soul" to a new enlightenment according to a sharply defined, ascending process.
Beginning from his sorry state as a helpless lover, chained to
his senses, the soul ascends, step by step, toward the contemplation of divine love. At each stage of the *scala*, the lover
realizes that his own efforts will propel him yet higher.
"[T]hrough the vertue of imagination," says Bembo, the
lover "shall fashion within himselfe that beautie much more
faire than it is in deede . . . hee will take this love for a stayre
(as it were) to climbe up to another far higher than it."[7]
Though its ultimate goal is the vision of "great universall
beautie," the regimen Bembo outlines does not utterly
disparage the life of the senses. Indeed, the doctrine of the
soul's progress presupposes an inherent goodness in sensuality; the flesh, properly governed, is exalted, in effect, as the
necessary means of attaining the joys of the spirit. When Colin finds in Cynthia "the image of the heauens in shape
humane" (*Colin Clout*, 351), he acknowledges the
neoplatonic affirmation that the attainment of spiritual joy
begins in the flesh. Love in man is a divinely ordained and
cosmically necessary movement upwards toward spiritual
perfection.

Love giveth unto the soule a greater happinesse. For like as through the particular beautie of one bodie hee guideth her to the universall beautie of all bodies: Even so in the least degree of perfection through particular understanding he guideth her to the universall understanding.[8]

Colin Clout's progress rehearses the classic ascent of the neoplatonic soul. In the *Calender* he begins falteringly, inadequately, but distinctly. His progress is implied more than achieved, but the portents are unmistakable: he is the neoplatonic lover *manqué*. Furthermore, his failure as a lover—and his later success in *Colin Clout*—is intimately related to his failure as a poet. As Piers reminds us in "October," Colin's inability to "bridle" his lover's passions thwarts his promise as a poet. In ways that I shall presently elaborate, Colin's personae as both poet and lover are almost thoroughly inclusive of one another. His progress as a poet accords intrinsically with his progress as a lover over the course of these two pastorals. This mutuality of roles derives, of course, from the accepted neoplatonic notions that the poet's goal is the same as that of the lover, and that his devotion to the Heavenly Venus can be the viable route along which he ascends to the contemplation of Beauty. But there is more to Colin's dual role than that truism; an insight into the poetic vocation that is peculiarly Spenserian and peculiarly pronounced in his pastorals is at work in the career of Colin Clout. This insight recognizes that the imagination is a faculty whose genesis is corporeal; it is given life and knowledge through the senses, furnished with the material of the natural world. The medium of the imagination is language, and it therefore shares with the senses—the lover's medium—a precarious fragility. Both language and the senses are easily corrupted, obviously a part of the fallen world of discord and danger, in need of the "gouvernaunce" and discipline of the aspiring soul. Colin's struggle over the course of these two pastorals reenacts the moral journey of the Spenserian poet through the perils of the world and chronicles his arduous ascent toward "universall understanding."

Although E. K.'s introduction and glosses often prove to be more trouble than they are worth, every reexamination of the *Calender* relies on them in coming to terms with the perplexities of the poem. The pedantry and faulty information that E. K. so laboriously provides, though, are subsidiary to the chief function of his notes, to strengthen the claim of the *Calender* to recognition as a significant statement of a significant poet. His defense of Spenser's choice of pastoral is worth quoting. Pastoral, he correctly maintains, is the endeavor of young poets eager to prove themselves,

> and as young birdes, that be newly crept out of the nest, by little first to prove theyr tender wyngs, before they make a greater flyght. So flew Theocritus, as you may perceive he was all ready full fledged. So flew Virgile, as not yet well feeling his winges. . . . So finally flyeth this our new Poete, as a bird, whose principals scarce growen out, but yet as that in time shall be hable to keepe wing with the best.
> ["Dedicatory Epistle," p. 10]

E. K.'s fussiness is amusing, but his figure of the poet as a bird is important, because it anticipates "October," where that metaphor is exploited more seriously as part of Piers's and Cuddie's debate on the value of poetry. The figure of the poet as a bird, capable of transcendent flight, has of course a long and complicated history from Plato onwards.[9] It also happens to be the figure that Bembo employs to describe neoplatonic lovers at an early stage of their progress, when they are "like to yong birdes almost flush, which for they flitter a litle their tender winges, yet dare not stray farre from the nest, nor commit themselves to the winde and open weather."[10]

It is not surprising, then, that when the metaphor of the bird makes its most pronounced appearance, late in "Oct-

ober," it refers to Colin as both a poet and a lover. In the
midst of a debate between Cuddie and Piers on the social and
moral value of "Pierlesse Poesye," the argument naturally
turns to Colin as a case in point. Love, Piers maintains, is
Colin's inspiration, the source of his poetic energy that
enables him to attain the gates of heaven:

> . . . loue does teach him climbe so hie,
> And lyftes him vp out of the loathsome myre:
> Such immortall mirrhor, as he doth admire,
> Would rayse ones mynd aboue the starry sky.
>
> [91-94]

But Cuddie disagrees with this optimistic analysis. He claims
that

> . . . it is all to weake and wanne,
> So high to sore, and make so large a flight:
> Her peeced pyneons bene not so in plight,
> For *Colin* fittes such famous flight to scanne:
> He, were he not with loue so ill bedight,
> Would mount as high, and sing as soote as Swanne.
>
> [83-90]

The disagreement stems from their different uses of the word
"loue." Cuddie's use implies bodily passion, lust, an enslav-
ing and demeaning force to which Colin, like all men, is
vulnerable. Piers, of course, uses the word in its neoplatonic
sense of a spiritual force capable of releasing the soul from its
imposed, fleshly condition. They articulate a discrepancy between, on one hand, freedom, flight, and inspiration; and, on
the other, control, constraint, and bondage. This divergence
constitutes two halves of a single controlling—and complex—metaphor that pervades the *Calender*, points toward
*Colin Clout*, and epitomizes the dilemma of the hero. The
dual metaphor of "constraint" and "flight" applies
simultaneously to Colin's roles as poet and lover; but it is fit-
ting and prudent to unravel the metaphor as it applies to Col-

in first as a poet, later as a lover.

"October," to nobody's surprise, employs the metaphor
most distinctly under the auspices of "poetry." In his defense
of the poet's calling, Piers repeatedly evokes an image of the
poet rising above his everyday circumstances. "Lyft vp thy
selfe out of the lowly dust" (37), he admonishes Cuddie, so
that "thy muse [may] display her fluttryng wing" (43). In this
way will "Cuddies name to Heaven sownde" (54). Piers also
uses opposing images of restraint and curtailment to describe
the poet's vocation, though these are not so noticeable as his
rhapsodies on poetic freedom and flight.

> O what an honor is it, to restrain
> The lust of lawlesse youth with good aduice
>
> [20-21]

he quite properly and nobly exclaims. And again:

> Soone as thou gynst to sette thy notes in frame
> O how the rurall routes to thee do cleave.
>
> [24-25]

Just as Orpheus "tame[d]" Cerberus, the poet tames his
"notes in frame."

Restraint, then, with regard to the poet's shaping and
organizing of his material, is not only virtuous, but an indispensable prerequisite of good poetry. This notion appears
repeatedly in the *Calender* whenever a shepherd poet makes
his appearance, pipe in hand. The poet is usually said to
"frame" a song, to organize his art under the power of his
skill. Of Colin Clout we are told immediately in "Januarye"
that "well couth he tune his pipe, and frame his stile" (10).
Colin tells Hobbinol in "June" that he intends his verse to be
rustic and rude because "the fytter they, my carefull case to
frame" (78). The metaphor of "framing" a verse echoes the
familiar notion, Sidney's in particular, of the poet as
"maker," one who constructs his poem like a craftsman with

his tools. The appearance of the poet as an artificer, ordering and controlling the passions and loftier flights of his talent (E. K.'s "diuine fury") through the medium of language, accords with my description in the previous chapter of the pastoral imagination's initial self-conscious constriction of setting, diction, subject, and characterization. For both Spenser and Milton, it will be remembered, these limitations imposed by the choice of pastoral inevitably evolve in the course of the poem into lofty utterances that transcend their humble origins.

In the *Calender* especially, we find this dialectic between restriction and flight, with regard to the poet's dual role as "maker" and *"vates,"* at unusually close quarters. When Colin is praised in "October," for instance, he is said to *"fitt* such famous *flight* to scanne"* (88) (my italics), so that both halves of the metaphor tug at one another in equipoise. And the Muses, who are often represented as perched on "Parnassus hight" ("June," 28), perform the same sort of controlling function, as we learn when Colin tells us in "December" that "the Muse so wrought me from my birth" (38). Even Colin's dead preceptor, Tityrus, though he now "Lyeth ywrapt in lead," nonetheless has achieved a form of ascent or release by means of his fame, which "doth dayly greater growe" ("June," 89, 92).

Although "flight" and "constraint" necessarily complement one another in the *Calender*, Spenser cautiously weighs the balance in favor of control and discipline as prerequisite to the poet's flight heavenward. (The "moral" eclogues, incidentally, demonstrate Spenser's obvious emphasis on "constraint.")[11] Even in the most workaday details of the shepherd-poet's life we see Spenser making use of the ordering and governing half of the metaphor. Colin himself tells us that he has achieved his high status as a poet among his peers because he was "wont to frame my pype/ Vnto the shifting of the shepheards foote" ("December," 115-6). We learn in "December" how profound Colin's discipleship to the landscape has been, for he has learned his song from the processes of nature around him. "I was wont to seeke the honey Bee,/ Working her formall rowmes in Wexen frame" (68-69),[12] he recounts, "[a]nd learned of lighter timber cotes to frame" (77). The repetition of the framing metaphor reminds us that Colin has tuned his song "vnto the Waters fall" ("Aprill," 36) and that his tutelage in the rhythms of the pastoral landscape has been responsible for the harmonies he can orchestrate.

We witness the rewards of Colin's poetic discipline, then, in moments that reveal feats nothing short of orphic. Hobbinol describes, for Colin's benefit, the wonders that Colin had been capable of before succumbing to Rosalind's unobtainable charms. It was Colin's song, he says,

> Whose Echo made the neyghbor groues to ring,
> And taught the byrds, which in the lower spring
> Did shroude in shady leaues from sunny rayes,
> Frame to thy songe their chereful chiriping,
> Or hold theyr peace, for shame of thy swete layes.
> ["June," 52-56]

In description that again evokes Orpheus, Hobbinol claims that he saw Calliope and her cohorts abandon their "yuory Luyts and Tamburins" (57) to rush toward Colin's ravishing strains, only to reach it and draw back,

> . . . as halfe with shame confound,
> Shepheard to see, them in theyr art outgoe.
> ["June," 63-64]

Hobbinol's vignette illustrates graphically Colin's gift for distilling in the alembic of his verse a product far surpassing the constraints of normal experience. Though he be bound to the stubborn requirements of his craft, as man is bound to the cycle of fallen nature, and the *Calender* itself is bound to its pastoral tradition and conventions, he works the miracles of his art within the very confines of that craft. His verse is capable of choreographing nature into harmonious patterns, as the shepherd poet himself stands piping in the center of creation. The Muses fall mute in wonderment before his song.

Hobbinol is in a good position to appreciate the loss of Colin's orphic powers; it is he who repeats Colin's song "Of Fayre *Eliza*, Queene of Shepheardes all" in "Aprill," a hymn composed before Colin had "plongd in payne" (12) for Rosalind. Aside from its many intrinsic virtues, the hymn has special significance, then, as both a reminder of Colin's former strength and a presage of his rehabilitation, fleeting in "November" and magnificent in *Colin Clout*. The eclogue also presents an aspect of Colin's "personality" that we do not find in quite the same way elsewhere in the *Calender*, although we will see it full-fledged in *Colin Clout*, that of the poet in command of a dramatic situation.

The hymn is constructed largely as a series of stage directions issued by Colin, who organizes—indeed, creates—the scene before our eyes. His song is a tissue of imperatives that coordinate nature and the pagan deities into orderly, repectful postures around the glorious person of the "Mayden Queene." The authoritative poet tells the nymphs to forsake their brook and instructs the Muses to help him "blaze/ Her worthy praise" (43-44). He directs the universe to "see, where she sits," and tells Cynthia to "shewe thy selfe . . . and be not abasht. (55, 82-83)." In alternate stanzas of the poem, Colin, whose power seems capable of structuring the entire landscape around the "Princesse . . . principall (126)," steps back and directs the attention of his audience to the scene he has created.[14] "Lo," he says proudly, "how finely the graces can it foote/ to the Instrument" (111). The picture he describes is one of a thoroughly ordered and governed structure with ladies ranged in rows, and nymphs arrayed in proper degree around the sovereign. The poet never allows the scene to act itself out, as it were, but stands before it, directing its participants imperially. "See that your rudenesse doe not you disgrace" (132), he warns the shepherdesses, as if he himself were not among their number. Having completed the task, Colin finally addresses Eliza and closes the hymn:

> Now ryse vp Elisa, decked as thou art,
>     in royall aray:
> And now ye daintie Damsells may depart
>     echeone her way.
> I fear, I haue troubled your troupes to longe:
> Let dame Eliza thank you for her song.
>     And if you come hether,
>     When Damsines I gether,
> I will part them all you among.

[145-53]

Colin introduces his earlier modest tone, even as he continues to command the participants in his masque-like production. It is he, after all, who bids Eliza rise, and he who dismisses the "daintie Damsells"—though Eliza herself is asked to thank them.[15]

The speaker whom we hear in "Aprill" is a far different shepherd from the mournful boy of "Januarye," the distraught lover of "June," and the embittered old man of "December." Spenser's presentation of Colin in a variety of guises indicates something important about his "spokesman." He wants us to follow the story of Colin's love for Rosalind—indeed, over the course of two poems. But Colin is not a character based on the conventions of narrative, not even the conventions the poet employs to create the major characters of the The Faerie Queene. Spenser urges us to inspect Colin's behavior from a variety of perspectives, all of which together tend to deflect interest away from the "personality" and toward his function as both a poet and a lover. Spenser's interest in Colin centers on how the poet-lover can and should act. This is why we find other shepherds, Colin's friends, able to repeat Colin's songs in his absence with perfect propriety, in "Aprill" and "August." This refusal to observe rigorous narrative (much less autobiographical) conventions best expresses Spenser's habit of exploring various aspects of the poet's life in his pastorals.

The most important aspect of the poet's life that the *Calender* examines is his love life. "Love" is Spenser's emblem in the *Calender* of the poet's creatureliness, his life as a flesh-and-blood being, the most compelling sign of his existence in a fallen world. If we direct our attention to Colin's attempt to deal with love, we find that Spenser treats the problem by means of the dual metaphor of "constriction/flight" and in a fashion similar to that which shapes his ideas about poetry. Love, like poetry, must be "framed" (when speaking of love Spenser usually uses the word "bridled") before it can surmount the crude imperatives of the flesh and achieve its fullest expression in an exalted vision. Colin's allegiance to the demands of his flesh preconditions his ultimate strength as a poet. Because he has "unbridled" his flesh, his poetry—while it may be of a high order—will not consistently attain its highest reaches.

Colin's problem in the *Calender* is not that he produces poor poetry. Even in his most exaggerated, self-regarding misery, he turns a good verse. His problem is that he is a poor lover and therefore cannot be a better poet. "Januarye" and "June," for example, are pleasing poems that engage our sensibilities in a variety of ways. But the performance of neither of these poems helps Colin to prevail over the confinements of his misery; these introverted meditations offer neither Colin nor anyone else a solution, an alternative to the woes of the lover. He remains morbidly egocentric, socially useless, sterile.

The sestina in "August" is an excellent case in point. The eclogue as a whole consists of two parts: the first is the playful song contest between Perigot and Willye, the second Colin's exquisite sestina, sung by Cuddie. The song contest,

harmless enough, hardly prepares us for the dolorous turn
that the eclogue takes when Colin's "heavy laye" (149)
begins. Like "Januarye," the sestina relies on the pathetic
fallacy; but unlike the initial eclogue, Colin's lament ought to
alarm us as we apprehend the depths to which he has plunged
in self-absorption. The shepherd's boy of "Januarye" amused us by finding a reflection of his unhappiness in the winter
landscape. There is nothing amusing about Colin's cry for the
perversion of nature itself:

> Let stremes of teres supply the place of sleep,
> Let all, that sweet is, voyd. . . .
>
> [163-64]

Now he perceives the landscape, resounding with "cryes"
and "shrieking sounds," as a fit place to "dwell apart" (167,
173, 169) in utter solitude, like some execrable beast, wailing
his pain into the night.

There is no question that, technically, the sestina is verse of a
high order, notable (as befits a sestina) for the aural power of
the end-words. The technical virtuosity, however, bears an
ironic relevance to the state of Colin's mind. He has indeed
framed his style, but certainly not his love. For the very
reason that the verse is the product of an exceptionally
energetic imagination, it emphasizes how seriously Colin has
introverted his talent to feed his own pain. And so, while with
Periogot we may say, "O Colin, Colin . . ./ How I admire
ech turning of thy verse" (190-91), we must further recognize
that his "turning" is directed inward, rather than upward; it
is vain and self-regarding, rather than beneficial and purposeful.

Colin himself is at least partly aware that his failure to
restrain his passion has directed his energies only within
himself: in "December" he asks "whether luck or loues
vnbridled lore" (63) has led him to his misery. Colin's

friends, though, understand more acutely that his failure to
govern passion has allowed passion to govern him, and
thereby has stymied his full poetic growth. Hobbinol
reproaches him directly:

Thy Muse to long slombreth in sorrowing,
Lulled a sleepe through loues misgouernaunce.
["November," 4-5]

And Thenot asks of him:

And hath he skill to make so excellent,
Yet hath so little skill to brydle loue?
["Aprill," 19-20]

Thenot's question points directly to the metaphorical connection that Spenser confects between love and poetry: can Colin
control ("make") verses and not control ("brydle") love?
The *Calender*'s answer is a melacholy "yes." Colin's friends
bewail the paradox, the sad incongruity, that a craftsman of
Colin's sublimity is unable to restrain his own destructive
passions.

We observe this paradox graphically in the initial and final
eclogues. In "Januarye" Colin looks to the landscape for
sympathy. Finding no comfort even in the "tears" of his
sheep, he destroys his minstrel's pipe, the very implement
that can lift him to heaven and relieve his pain. By a bizarre
twist of logic, he proclaims that, because Rosalind scorns his
music, his music must cease to exist; he blames his poetry for
his failure to achieve the inner control of the mature lover.
After an unrequited year of bitterness and disappointment,
Colin, as an old man in "December," once again abandons
his pipe. Still suffering from a cancerous love for Rosalind,
he recounts his life in the last eclogue with reference to two
entwined activities: his enterprise as a poet and as a lover.
Love, he admits, gave him checkmate and withered the
fragrant flowers of his poetry. "Ah who," he asks,

. . . has wrought my Rosalind this spight
To spil the flowres, that should her garland dight?

[113-114]

His final abandonment of his pipe signals his final
discouragement with the power of his song to melt Rosalind's
icy heart. As he bids the world adieu, he clings to the belief
that he has failed as a poet because he has failed as a lover.
But we know otherwise. If Colin fails as a poet at all, it is not
because he produces bad poetry, but because his belief in his
powers has been corrupted by his poisonous obsession with
Rosalind.

We know otherwise, because we have just witnessed, in
"November," the measure of Colin's imaginative might and
the surest portent of his triumph in *Colin Clout*. The elegy for
Dido is the only eclogue in which we see Colin in live performance, so to speak, practicing his art before his compatriots
in his own person. In Spenser's delineation of the portrait of
the artist, the elegy is absolutely central to the whole collection. And yet, compared to "Aprill" or to any of the other
eclogues where Colin appears, the persona he adopts is
relatively colorless, unobtrusive of idiosyncrasy or
"character." Furthermore, unlike elsewhere in the *Calender*,
we are relatively unaware of him as the lover of Rosalind. (In
fact, Rosalind is barely mentioned (1. 17), though Thenot
accuses Colin on "loues misgouernaunce." [4])    Finally,
"November" is the most patently "literary" eclogue in the
collection. As a pastoral elegy, whose forebears stretch with
great distinction from Theoritus and Virgil to Marot and Petrarch, "November" asks to be measured against a redoubtable
tradition. It abides by virtually every convention of its mode,
from the invocation of the Muses, to the questioning of the
rural deities and the final consolation. More than anywhere
else in the *Calender*, then, Colin proves that by rigorous
observance of the demands of his craft, and by discipline over
his human frailties, he is capable of a visionary utterance that

helps explain to his peers the mysteries of life and death.

Colin undertakes his dirge at Thenot's request that the poet create for his fellow shepherds a monumental song "whose endles souenaunce/ Emong the shepeheards swaines may aye remaine" (5-6). His opening cry to Melpomene, the "mournefulst Muse of nyne," signals that his adherence to the conventions of his art can lead him out of the self-entrapment of the sestina. The relentlessly successive stanzas, metrically intricate, consolingly ritualistic, enact the momentum of his harnassed imagination. He begins slowly, but resolutely; throughout the early part of the elegy he assumes a philosophical and interrogatory posture:

> Why doe we longer liue (ah why liue we so long?)
> Whose better dayes death hath shut vp in woe?
>
> [73-74]

Each ten-line stanza, concluded with a refrain ("O heauie hearse. . . . O carefull verse."), introduces a different topic following logically upon the one before it. Leading its audience in an almost liturgical progression, he steadily ascends to the final apotheotic vision (163-72). Dido is not dead, but simply "unbodied" of her fleshly mortality. His poetic gifts have provided him with the means of ascent, the ladder to the vision that, in his love life, he is incapable of achieving. Speaking with prophetic fervor for the benefit of the audience around him, Colin finally reaches his goal:

> I see thee blessed soule, I see,
> Walke in *Elisian* fieldes so free.
>   O happy herse,
> Might I once come to thee (O that I might)
>   O ioyful verse.
>
> [178-82]

Colin's act of public performance—and this is public performance *par excellence*—actively transmutes grief to joy.

Bound and "framed" to the exigencies of its conventions, Colin's elegy, by the very means of its inherent, formal restrictions, succeeds as one of his most splendid utterances. If the *Calender* had ended here—if Dido's elegy had been "December"— we would be left with the comforting portrait of an artist who seems finally to have overcome his infirmities, to have directed his energies away from his own monomania toward a noble career in the service of his fellowmen. But such a conclusion would violate the overall impact that has accumulted through the eclogues. Spenser places "November" *before* yet another dispiriting glimpse of Colin in the final eclogue, because, as always, he refuses to provide easy solutions. Like the struggle of Everyman, Colin's struggle will not be won with a single leap. Spenser places "November" in the penultimate position in the *Calender* as a glimpse of what the poet, even in the midst of his misery and despair as a lover, could accomplish were he to surmount his weaknesses. After all, Orpheus himself, Colin's mythic forebear, though he could tame nature and charm Pluto, could not make the ascent from Hades without succumbing to his passions:

> . . . And now they were within
> A kenning of the upper earth, when Orphye did begin
> To dowt him lest shee followed not, and through an eager
>     love
> Desyrous for to see her he his eyes did backward move.
> Immediately shee slipped backe.[17]

Colin Clout's "eager love," his failure to master the sinister "wandring way" ("December," 62) of his fleshly desires, causes him to "backward move" in "December." The responsible poet's art is life-encompassing; this is why the *Calender* is not really completed until Colin has encompassed more of life, until Eliza, Dido, and Rosalind assume their harmonious and just places in his imaginative life.

In *Colin Clouts Come Home Againe* Spenser reincarnates the love-smitten and isolated shepherd, whom we leave in "December," with all the "aspyring wit" of a confident poet in full self-possession. Insofar as the entire action of the poem centers fully on Colin's career as a poet-lover, Spenser eliminates many of the concerns of the *Calender*, most noticeably (and for most readers, most happily) the satire against ecclesiastical abuse. He frees himself from the type of variety that the eclogue form required and instead draws many of the strands of the earlier poem into a unified narration of the affairs of Colin Clout. Seeming to spring almost on a trajectory from the *Calender*, the course of *Colin Clout* ascends relentlessly, not only in terms of situation and theme, but also by means of the poem's various tropes and rhetorical figures. The poem presents an organic and ascending series of fictions as it chronicles Colin's emergence from the pastoral world to the courtly and from there to the revelation of the cosmic process. In guiding our reponse to his life's journey, Colin fulfills the promise that he only tentatively and momentarily held out in the *Calender*. In this poem we watch him as he disburdens himself and climbs toward a fresh understanding of man's life in the world.

It is important to recognize immediately, however, that Colin has not by any means disburdened himself of his carnal needs and compulsions. At the end of the poem, he is still in love with Rosalind and has as little hope of being requited as he had in the *Calender*. He still faces the fleshly lover's "paine which cannot be recured" (946). But his poetry has provided him the pathway out of his earlier sterile self-absorption to an acceptance of his state and to the wisdom that makes his pain endurable. His poetic gifts help him to see in Rosalind's bodily beauty the "diuine regard and heauenly hew"(933) that makes the ache of sensuality meaningful. At the end of the poem he knows that his "praise" (942), his poetic celebration of the beauty Rosalind incarnates, will bring him "grace":

Such grace shall be some guerdon for the griefe,
And long affliction which I have endured.

[943-44]

*Colin Clout* recounts the process of his arrival at the point where he can accept and make sense of the pain of being human. His struggle continues to be the same struggle he waged—and lost—in the *Calender*. Then, his powers were nearly destroyed by love. Now, his imagination will guide him up the *scala* to share his vision with his fellowmen.

Spenser's insistence on the centrality of "poetry," on its power as a medium toward truth, is animated by the very variety of roles that Colin assumes in the poem. His various personae as shepherd, lover, aspiring courtier, moral philosopher, and, ultimately, as rhapsode embody the contexts in which we are to read the poem and ponder its values. For *Colin Clout* is nothing if not a poem of values. It asks us to inspect an assortment of situations—the bucolic life, for example, or the life of the courtier, or love both human and divine—according to the criteria provided by Colin's moral sense. The poem persuades us that the responsible poet can illuminate in his verse the "right way" among the everyday choices that as moral beings we are bound to confront. By having Colin Clout confront and act upon such choices, according to the insights that the shepherd's own imagination has given him access to, Spenser accomplishes a double feat. Colin's insistent reference of his own experience to the norms provided by "poetry" makes his art not only the unique entry to the summum bonum but also the practicable means of judging and discriminating among the diversities of mundane life. The poem vigorously affirms the imagination's adequacy to comprehend this multifarious world as a unified whole and, at the same time, to live with its multiplicity more happily.

As if to deny the grandeur of my foregoing claims for it, the poem begins rather casually, with a vignette of Colin "[c]harming his oaten pipe vnto his peres" (5). But our attention is quickly directed to the importance of Colin's coming home again, his reintegration into the life of the pastoral world. The tired swain we left in the *Calender*, his pipe abandoned on a tree, has now resumed his responsibility as the leader of the rustic swains,

> Who all the while with greedie listfull eares,
> Did stand astonisht at his curious skill,
> Like hartless deare, dismayed with thunders sound.
>
> [8-10]

The effect of Colin's "curious skill" evokes Orpheus, enchanting the animate and inanimate with his primordial rhythms. In fact, throughout the first lines of the poem, before Colin has even spoken, the myth of Orpheus emerges in its most triumphant form. By associating Colin with Orpheus's religious powers, Spenser wastes no time in preconditioning our reception of his hero. Hobbinol spends over ten lines describing to Colin the poet's importance to the vitality of the landscape:

> Whilest thou was hence, all dead in dole did lie
> The woods were heard to waile full many a sythe,
> And all their birds with silence to complaine . . .
> But now both woods and fields, and floods reviue,
> Sith thou art come, their cause of meriment,
> That vs late dead, has made againe alive.
>
> [22-31]

By equating the return of Colin with the return of life, Hobbinol exceeds the usual hyperbole of the pathetic fallacy and prepares us for the oracular moments to come later. The aspect of the Orpheus myth that was adumbrated in "Aprill" will be augmented in *Colin Clout* by other legends attached to the Thracian bard, specifically his role as priest and prophet that the Italian neoplatonists found so congenial.[18]

When Colin begins his account of his adventures, though, he seems to undermine the expectation that has mounted in the early lines of the poem. Far from evoking an image of Orpheus, his recollection of his lonely life evokes merely his sorry portrait in the *Calender*. He tells how his capacity for purposeful song had languished while he pined for the unattainable Rosalind:

> For loue had me forlorne, forlorne of me,
> That made me in that desart chose to dwell.
>
> [90-91]

This self-imposed exile in the desert clashes with the picture that the opening of the poem presents of Colin surrounded by his friends in the center of their society. Between the two episodes lies Colin's visit to the court. The vision of Cynthia that he witnessed there has wrenched him from his lonely and fruitless obsession with Rosalind and has provided him with a mission. He must sing the praises of the Queen:

> Wake then my pipe, my sleepie *Muse* awake,
> Till I haue told her prises lasting long.
>
> [48-49]

His recollection of his "lifes sole bliss" (47) has given him a renewed social purpose, to recreate his vision of "that Angel . . . heauens fairest light" (40-41) for his bucolic compatriots. Colin's powers as a poet find beneficent expression in his encomium to Cynthia, and his attempts to re-create his "sight" (43) of her constitute what he takes to be his life's purpose.

Throughout the long and often immoderate catalogue of Cynthia's virtues, however, it becomes clear that Colin's praise of her constitutes more than simply an acclamation of her "power, her mercy, and her wisdome" (346). His poetic recreation of her in all her glory testifies just as strongly to his own formidable ability to embody this paragon. By presen-

ting his adulation as the very vessel of her incomparable
goodness, Colin dramatically ensures his own authority. Furthermore, he magnifies the respect of his audience for his
skills by his repeated protestations of inadequacy to the
chore.[19] As one of his listeners innocently perceives,

> . . . By wondring at thy *Cynthiaes* praise
> *Colin*, thy selfe thou mak'st vs to wonder,
> And her vpraising, doest thy selfe vpraise.
>
> [353-55]

Colin's encomium to Cynthia, then, establishes his moral
prestige and in so doing paves the way for his later arresting
pronouncements. More immediately, Colin's celebration of
Cynthia proclaims itself to be an act of lasting value, an utterance that will long outlive its speaker and circumstances.
Colin himself admits as much when, after his final diapason
of Cynthia's beatitudes (590-615), even his admiring listeners
are taken aback by his extravagance, and they reproach him
for "mount[ing] so hie" (617). Colin resists this censure,
though, on the grounds that "[h]er name recorded will I
leaue for euer" (631). His poetic record of her virtues will
bestow upon Cynthia an immortality that might otherwise be
lost:

> And long while after I am dead and rotten,
> Amongst the shepheardes daughters dancing round,
> My layes made of her shall not be forgotten,
> But sung by them with flowry gyrlonds crownd.
>
> [640-43]

His power, then, is twofold: not only can he perpetuate for
all ages the virtue of Cynthia in his verse, but that very verse
secures his own immortality. No longer does he merely aspire
to be worthy of glorifying Cynthia's name, but he prophesies
what "will" be the effect of his art in future ages. Gradually,
Colin is ascending to the orphic heights intimated in the

poem's opening lines. By the end of the section of the poem that celebrates the courtly ideal, Colin has earned the respect of the reader, so that Spenser's audience and Colin's rural listeners are now united in positive disposition towards the poet's teachings. Colin is therefore free to adopt a more authoritative posture. The shepherd swain has become the social arbiter and turns his attention next to the excoriation of vice in the courtly world.

A word ought to be said first about Colin's praise of the poets and "nymphes" whom he encountered during his stay at court. This section of the poem (376-583) has long served as a treasure trove of contemporary allusions and is indeed of interest on that account.[21] It is Colin's relationship to the courtiers, however, that bears examination, if this section of the poem has a justifiable, organic role in the poem as a whole. The lines are introduced when Alexis questions whether Cynthia bestowed her kindness on Colin, this "simple silly Elfe" (371), because the host of shepherds who already wait on her are not worthy of the name of poets. Colin protests this accusation by praising a number of these poets, some of whom are easily recognized figures from Elizabeth's court. Poetry itself is a highly esteemed endeavor in Cynthia's land, because:

> There learned arts do florish in great honor,
> And Poets wits are had in peerlesse price.
>
> [320-21]

The great Shepherdess herself has "peerlesse skill in making well" (188) and has provided the nursery in which poetry might flourish. He emphasizes specific qualities that Cynthia's poets possess and measures the achievement of each according to his attainment of one or more of these attributes. First there is skill: he praises one poet because he could "pipe himselfe with passing skill" (443); he encourages another to raise "his tunes from laies to matter of more skill"

(394). Then there is tradition and fame. One poet, Colin claims, is capable of producing a poem surpassing that of "Po and Tyburs swans" and "all the brood of Greece so highly praised" (412-13). When a poet is "fit to frame an everlasting dittie" (385), no longer will his "fame lie so in hidden shade" (407), but it will immortalize him. The primary motive behind all good poetry, Colin implies, is the reaching after perfection, an enterprise he characterizes, as we might have predicted, in terms of height. He encourages poets to climb, to "raise" their tunes (394), and to "lift" their notes "vnto their wonted height" (390). The result will be that poetry will be "to the pitch of . . . perfection raised" (415) and will "their *Cynthia* immortall make" (453).

Colin's attitude toward the state of poetry in Cynthia's court accords with the new posture of authority and self-confidence he is developing through the poem. Simple silly elf he may be, but he nevertheless has a judicious remark extending beyond mere opinion for each of the poets that he mentions. Nor does he simply describe their achievements. His intent is to commend and criticize, but from a position that implies superiority. He encourages the poets to develop their talents and to write in a higher vein. His consistent emphasis on "height" in fact implies a physical separation between Colin and the courtly poets, whereby it is the lowly swain who encourages the courtiers to tax their talents to attain *his* position. After all, Cynthia has chosen Colin from her retinue of loyal poets to sing her praises and elevate her name. In effect, then, Colin's generous praise of his courtly fellows confers authority on himself and strengthens his own claim to the guardianship of the Muses. He immediately demonstrates his capabilities as a superbly courteous poet by issuing a lengthy encomium to the ladies of the court. He describes them in only slightly less beatific terms than Cynthia herself, with the expected Petrarchan and neoplatonic trappings in full deployment. Where, though, can one find such overused imagery so skillfully set forth as in these lines?:

*Phylis* the floure of rare perfection,
Faire spreading forth her leaues with fresh delight,
That with their beauties amorous reflexion,
Bereaue of sence each rash beholders sight.

[544-47]

The section of the poem that relies most obviously on the
tradition that pastoral may employ disguises to glance at
greater matters is the one which exposes the realities of courtly vice. In this section Colin argues that essentially beneficial
values have been perverted by many in Cynthia's court, making it no sort of place for a simple shepherd. A "guilefull
hollow hart" often is "masked with faire dissembling
curtesie" (699-700). Spenser's method of portraying the evil
side of courtly life is a skillful one. He reverses the benign images that he employed in praising the courtly poets in order to
demonstrate how grossly those values have been abused.
Hence, we are presented with the negative equivalent of the
height imagery used earlier:

. . . each one seeks with malice and with strife,
To thrust downe other into foule disgrace,
Himselfe to raise: and he doth soonest rise
That best can handle his deceitfull wit.

[690-93]

Malicious self-seeking motivates the false type of elevation
and aspiration that Colin condemns in this aspect of the life
he witnessed abroad. These false courtiers, "puffed vp with
pride" (759), travesty the aspiring poets praised earlier. In
fact, Colin castigates the abusers of the courtly ideal most
strongly for their shameful, debasing abuse of language,
reminding us in yet another way that *Colin Clout* is pervasively a poem about poetry. Unlike the skilled makers who aspire
to the school of learning, the unvirtuous courtier has a "filed
toung furnisht with tearmes of art" (701). The true poet
earlier who seeks to serve the Muse with "laies of love" is
here implicitly contrasted with the baser lovers whose

. . . walls and windows there are writ,
All full of loue, and loue, and loue my deare.

[776-77]

Colin's disgust derives from a superior wisdom provided him
by his talents as a poet. He knows that these false poets
pervert the love "whose seruice high so basely they ensew"
(767). Colin invokes, that is, both to praise and to blame, the
genuine criteria of good poetry, hence of true virtue. Good
poets and elevating poetry are the concomitants of virtue; the
enemies of virtue are the enemies of genuine poetry. In a
description that recalls the defeat of Orgoglio, Colin exposes
these "poet-apes":

For highest lookes haue not the highest mynd,
Nor haughtie words most full of highest thoughts:
But are like bladders blowen vp with wynd,
That being prickt do vanish into noughts.

[715-18]

Because Colin's strictures are so clearly the product of a
fervent concern for the overthrow of vice and the implemen-
tation of virtue, we do not doubt the righteousness of his con-
victions nor the propriety of his invective. Like the rural
group gathered around him, we accept what he presents not
only because he has, after all, seen it, but because his motives
are so indisputably worthwhile. His status as an outsider to
the court having prohibited any selfish interest, he never
descends to ad hominem attack or waspish abuse. His impar-
tiality sanctifies his condemnation; his fair and generous
recognition of whatever virtue there is ensures his authority.
Colin's consistent grounding of his moral judgments on the
criteria provided by the noble role of verse making makes his
pronouncements, as the poem proceeds, increasingly olympian.

It is with a natural decorum, therefore, that at the end of
the section on courtly vice, Colin launches a yet more grave
denunciation against the debasers of Love:

For with lewd speeches and licentious deeds,
His mightie mysteries they do prophane,
And vse his ydle name to other needs,
But as a complement for courting vaine.
So to him they do not serue as they professe,
But make him serue to them for sordid vses,
Ah my dread Lord, that doest liege hearts possesse,
Auenge thy selfe on them for their abuses.

[787-94]

Colin's direct address to the god of Love signals that he is preparing for his climactic neoplatonic hymn to love as the cosmic harmonizer. And his diction is changing accordingly. These courtly idolators are guilty of "lewd" speech (recalling that their vices constitute a corruption of poetry), and of profaning love's "mightie mysteries." Colin has taken upon himself an awesome new role that allows him to invoke the "dread Lord" in avengement of sin. His shepherd's weeds have been pretty well discarded, as he prepares to ascend the high altar of love.

Colin's rhapsodic revelation of love's true nature and genesis is neatly divided into two distinct sections (799-821; 839-95), separated by an interruption by Cuddy. Earlier (616-19), Cuddy rebuked Colin for his neglect of pastoral decorum in his "loftie flight" in praise of Cynthia. Now the note of rebuke has vanished, as Cuddy reveals his awe of the poet's oracular power:

Shepheard it seemes that some celestiall rage
Of loue (quoth Cuddy) is breath'd into thy brest,
That powreth forth these oracles so sage,
Of that high powre, wherewith thou art possest.
But neuer wist I till this present day
Albe of loue I alwayes humbly deemed,
That he was such an one, as thou doest say,
And so religiously to be esteemed.
Well may it seeme by this thy deep insight,
That of God the Priest thou shouldest bee:

So well thou wot'st the mysterie of his might,
As if his godhead thou didst present see.

[823-33]

Cuddy's enthusiasm helps us to receive Colin's teachings as an emblem of the poet in full possession of his might. While his "celestiall rage" recalls the "diuine fury" that was envisioned for Colin in the *Calender*, Cuddy's reaction ascribes an almost indomitably religious power to the poet. "Aprill" and "November" intimated what the ideal poet, unhampered by the "loathesome myre" of lust, might achieve in his flight to heaven. Now Colin approaches his goal. He has been "possest" by lofty love and now serves that god by instructing his fellow mortals in the "mysterie of his might." Cuddy boldly and unequivocally proclaims Colin the Priest of the God Love.

Acknowledging the justness of Cuddy's observations, Colin takes the mantle of high office onto his shoulders: "Indeed," says Colin, love "needs his priest t'expresse his power diuine" (838). His roles as oracle, teacher, mythmaker, and holy priest converge as he elucidates the genesis of love in the garden of Adonis and love's power in the shaping of human experience. Once again, we are asked to recall the myth of Orpheus, this time in the neoplatonic role of theologian and teacher of the occult, the role foreshadowed by the poem's opening lines on the necessity of Colin's song to the vitality of the landscape.[21] Now Colin has effectively left his time-bound, material circumstances far behind. His vatic powers have transported him to a vision of "Beautie the burning lamp of heauens light" (872) in a rapture that would have overawed Ficino himself. Finally, having limned the vision of universal truth, he concludes with a statement of practical morality that acknowledges the "wound" and "secret sence" (876, 886) of human passion but urges a "chaste heart" for "all louers." (887, 888). Colin's artistry has divined man's highest aspirations, beauty and love, and has figured them forth as moral virtues; or, as one of his listeners says, "with wondrous skill/ Has Cupid selfe depainted in his kynd" (897-89).

Perhaps the poem could very well have ended at this point. Having dissolved into ecstasies, in the fashion of Il Penseroso, and brought all heaven before our eyes, Colin could have concluded quite simply, content with this grand flourish of neoplatonic bravura. Instead, Colin returns to a point similar to that at which we first met him in "Januarye," forlorne of the ever-resistant Rosalind. He holds as little hope of winning her now, for all his poetic feats, as he did in "December." What has changed, though, is nothing less than his disposition toward life. His imagination has taught him how to endure the inescapable, riddling pain of mortality. Having had access to truths that only his poetry could provide, he now recognizes that the flesh and the spirit are intimately united, the spirit immanent in the flesh. His imagination has grasped the presence of "diuine regard and heauenly hew" (933) in the body of a woman he adores also with his "sence" (886).

At the end of *Colin Clout* the enterprises of poetry and love—with all the complexity and nuance that these endeavors signify—continue to define Colin's humanity, as they have through both poems. His poetic quest must always remain as elusive as the perfection of humanity, never to be achieved; "diuine regard" must always remain just beyond his formidable grasp,

> . . . sith I may not her loue:
> Yet that I may her honour paravent,
> And praise her worth, though far my wit aboue.
> [939-42]

Colin's privilege as a poet capable of penetrating the distant regions of the divine realm has blessed him with an awesome skill and cursed him with the realization that he will never fully see its fruition. The measure of his might lies in his effort.

# 3

## Milton's Early Pastorals

*W*hen *Poems of Mr. John Milton, Both English and Latin* appeared in 1645, the Stationer in his preface harbingered the volume as "bringing into the light as true a Birth, as the Muses have brought forth since our famous *Spencer* wrote; whose Poems in these English ones are as rarely imitated, as sweetly excell'd."[1] The tacit challenge to the reader to compare this new poet with his most renowned predecessor, a challenge similar to the one E. K. had issued with greater extravagance on behalf of his own new poet some sixty years earlier, has rarely been taken very seriously.[2] There is justness in this critical timidity; the extent of Spenser's influence on Milton's early work virtually defies verification, although we often cannot fail to overhear a Spenserian echo when Milton employs diction which by the middle of the seventeenth century had become old-fashioned, quaint, and associated with Spenser's numerous "followers."[3] Brooks and Hardy some years ago concluded sensibly and frankly that Spenser's "pastoralism" did in fact make its way into Milton's minor poems: "How much of it Milton did actually find in Spenser is hard to say. But certainly it was a great deal."[4] It seems far

75

less fruitful to explore the extent of Spenser's "influence" on the early Milton or to identify scattered uses of language that suggest a Spenserian "borrowing" than to approach Milton's first volume from the perspective on the poetic vocation that illuminates Spenser's pastorals. For there is no doubt, as Louis Martz has demonstrated, that the edition is arranged with great care, the poems are studiously "early" poems aimed at conveying "a sense of the predestined bard's rising powers."[5] The volume is also imbued with pastoral motifs, emblems, and situations that share with Spenser's pastorals the poet's self-conscious craving for a literary space in which to define and assess the poetic vocation itself.

But from here we must proceed gingerly. Milton's chief deviation from the Spenserian pastoral derives from the slippery principle that the pastoral mode itself is rather an outlook than a strict genre. With the important exception of *Lycidas*, he wrote no unequivocally English pastoral that demands attention primarily under the auspices and conventions of the "kind," and it is therefore rarely self-evident that we can extensively criticize Milton as a pastoral poet. Perhaps his refusal to limit himself, after the fashion of Spenser, to a thorough treatment of pastoral (say, in a series of eclogues) explains why Milton's use of the mode has not attracted the extensive scrutiny that would seem inescapable with respect to a poet so richly glossed and criticized. Nonetheless, in the early poems Milton steered a course that rarely took him far from pastoral.[6] His awareness of the tradition as one of the great European poetic expressions penetrated his imagination, making pastoral an integral habit of his poetic impulse. But although he consistently summons up pastoral situations, devices, language, and decorum, he does so rarely with an eye to conscious imitation—of Spenser or of anyone else—but more often as an imaginative reflex. This reflex often seems to submerge the overt manifestations of pastoral; he exploits the mode in a sense analogous to that in which pastoral exploits nature: he transfigures, submerges, metamorphoses the tradition to express a special insight that often seems far removed from the original source. That insight, as the early poems show, reveals pastoral as a fiction in which to explore the life of the poetic imagination in a fallen world. That Milton accomplishes this self-evaluating enterprise in ways markedly more subtle and complex than Spenser's employment of Colin Clout as his pastoral persona does not diminish the affinity of both poets for pastoral as a literary vehicle capable of construing the poet's place in life.

To determine the pastoral attitudes that the two poets share we may take instruction from juxtaposing the frontispiece of the 1645 volume, Milton's pictorial debut as a poet, against the woodcut that precedes "Januarye," introducing Colin Clout to the public.[7] The woodcut that opens the *Calender* presents the poet up close, but in full disguise as the shepherd's boy, Colin Clout, "[u]nder which name," E. K. helpfully informs us, "this Poete secretly shadoweth himself." The woodcut, not to mention E. K.'s paraphernalia, invites the reader into a landscape presided over by a poet pretending to be a shepherd. The frontispiece to Milton's first volume presents quite another picture of the poet. The engraving depicts a somber gentleman, looking rather older than his years, dressed in the clothing of a Londoner of the 1640s, and surrounded on four sides by the Muses. He squarely faces his reader from inside a room, and stands with his back to a half-curtained window that reveals a distant landscape, peopled by a shepherd and shepherdess dancing to a piping minstrel. Both pictures indicate that in some way the poet regards himself, or that his poems present him, in relation to the pastoral landscape. Like Colin Clout, Milton finds in the remote landscape an emblematic context, sanctified by tradition as appropriate to the novice, in which to introduce the artist to the public.

The differences between the two pictures, though, tellingly prepare us for the divergence between the poets' attitudes toward pastoral. Milton's distance from the rural scene that the reader glimpses over the poet's shoulder betokens his detachment from not only the landscape but also the pastoral poetry traditionally embodying the landscape. This crucial Miltonic "detachment" can be estimated justly if we recall Colin's attachment to the landscape, to the rhythms of which he tuned his pipe. In the last chapter we saw how intimately Colin's relation to the landscape hinged upon his vicissitudes as a lover. His long attempt to demarcate his poetic identity was contingent upon his mastery of "love," Spenser's unique expression of Colin's fallen creatural status. Colin's relation to the landscape and his ability to attune himself to its processes varied according to the degree of success with which he grappled with his inescapable fleshly weaknesses. In a fashion definitively Spenserian, Colin's career enacted the unremitting clash between the flesh and the spirit, with the attainment, at the end of *Colin Clout*, of the wisdom that poetry illuminates the hidden continuum of the flesh and the spirit, of nature and the spirit.

Milton's early poet-speakers, on the other hand, share almost none of Colin's frailty as creatures susceptible to the pain of sensuality. His poets consistently externalize the inevitable corruption of fallen life, so that for Milton the locus of natural corruption is detached from the poet's own status as a fallen creature. Fallen nature in Milton's early poems finds expression not in an internal, personal infirmity, but rather in an external corruption endemic to the landscape itself. The Miltonic pastoral poet, then, interprets his vocation not as struggle within himself, as Colin did, but as the clash of the righteous poet with the fallen world. We do not discover, as we did in Colin's career, an ascending personal regimen of a man in contest with his own weakness; but instead, we find that the Miltonic poet has shifted the struggle against natural infirmity to the poet's struggle against the landscape of pastoral itself. By this rather brittle and as yet unsubtantiated statement, I mean that Milton overgoes Spenser, as we followed him in Colin's progress, by summoning up pastoral as an image of fallen life, in order ultimately to reject it in favor of higher forms of spiritual experience which discredit participation in the realm of fallen life. Furthermore, by discrediting pastoral, the emblem of fallen nature, Milton simultaneously rejects pastoral as a literary mode, to be transcended in pursuit of the "higher argument" that constitutes his lifelong preoccupation.

The portrait of the Miltonic poet I am sketching is not an unfamiliar one, thanks not only to the biographical scholars among Milton's commentators, but also to the autobiographical fragments of Milton's prose and early "exercises." In fact, no better approach to the differences between Spenser's and Milton's pastoral imaginations can be found than in the famous preface to the second book of *The Reason of Church-Government* (1642). In spelling out his poetic aspirations, Milton exactly reverses the process of artistic self-definition that we saw Colin Clout enact in his career, whereby the poet achieved exalted, ennobling visions only *after* laborious personal and professional discipline. Milton's source of poetic truth is not bound as utterly to craftsmanship and personal self-control as it is to the "inspired gift of God rarely bestowed." He reveals, in a celebrated passage, that he hopes to attain his vision

> by devout prayer to that eternal Spirit who can enrich with all utterance and knowledge, who sends out his seraphim with the hallowed fire of his altar, to touch and purify the lips of whom he pleases. *To this must be added* industrious and select reading, steady observation, insight into all seemly and generous arts and affairs. [my italics][8]

Milton's artistry begins after his lips have been purified by the fire that touched Isaiah. For Colin, spiritual experience came as the reward of self-discipline and continued "insight into all seemly and generous arts and affairs."

My point here, of course, is deliberately exaggerated. I am certainly not about to deny Milton's faith in the value of practical experience, personal austerity, and wide learning as the fundamentals of the poetic vocation. But these necessary attributes augment Milton's deeper belief in himself as the vessel of religious and moral truth, capable of leading his fellowman toward spiritual regeneration. Professor Haller states the matter eloquently:

> His rebirth in the spirit started with the discovery of the spiritual function of poetry. It turned upon his discovery in himself of the power of poetic utterance, and it led to his decision to make poetry rather than the pulpit his weapon in the war of the spirit. Poems were to be his sermons, and his life was to be a poem.[9]

The effect of Milton's repeated sense of self-assurance cannot be separated from his treatment of pastoral, where his poetic life receives such complex treatment. There seems to be no doubt, despite his long search for a suitable poetic subject, that Milton never questioned his singularity, his unique place in the world. The preface states most clearly what we hear throughout Milton's writings, that he stands as the unique spiritual descendent of Orpheus, Virgil, Jeremiah, and St. John, that his poetry is "of power beside the office of a pulpit, to inbreed and cherish in a great people the seeds of virtue . . . to celebrate in glorious and lofty hymns the throne and equipage of God's almightiness, and what he works."[10]

In the light of Milton's exalted conception of his singular vocation we can best understand how pastoral, whether as an emblem of fallen life or as a literary form, represents an aspect of experience that must be transcended by the heroic imagination striving for regeneration. Just as the natural world for all its loveliness can only faintly suggest the inexpressible joys that await the soul in heaven, pastoral poetry represents only a stage in the inspired poet's goal to be doctrinal and exemplary to a nation. So while Milton perceives with Spenser the value of pastoral as a self-defining mode of utterance, he cuts his shepherd's weeds to his own fashion, and proceeds a characteristic step further. Pastoral as a self-reflective literary mode and pastoral as a representation of *natura naturata* are united in Milton's canon by virtue of their common inadequacy. Whether as an emblem of fallen life or as a literary form, pastoral can be valued only as a promise of a more exalted environment or a more glorious vision. Milton takes Spenser's self-conscious pastorals to an extreme by exploiting the mode as a creed outworn, as a preliminary stage in the evolution of the redeemed imagination.

Lest I be suspected of trying to reconjure the gloomy Milton whom his more hostile critics have presented, it seems important, before demonstrating how these observations can animate the early poems, to take note of the obvious: namely, that Milton never goes so far as to abhor or even to disesteem either pastoral poetry or the beauties of nature that pastoral exploits. After all, few readers of Milton can envisage Eden in many ways significantly different from the garden Milton has bequeathed us. It is equally commonplace, on the other hand, to remember that the truly perfect environment in *Paradise Lost* is heaven, and that Eden, though more masterfully realized, figures forth but a "shadow" of the "eternal Paradise of rest" (*Paradise Lost* 12. 314).[11] We can locate a more reasonable indication of what can only be called Milton's distrust of pastoral in Satan's expert pastoral vignette at the very climax of the epic, when, making his way into Eve's heart, he "gloz'd . . . and his Proem tun'd" (9. 549):

> . . . on a day roaving the field, I chanc'd
> A goodly Tree farr distant to behold
> Loaden with fruit of fairest colours mixt,
> Ruddie and Gold: I nearer drew to gaze;
> When from the boughes a savorie odour blow'n,
> Grateful to appetite, more pleas'd my sense
> Then of sweetest Fennel or the Teats

Of Ewe or Goat dropping with Milk at Eevn,
Unsuckt of Lamb or Kid, that tend thir play.

[9. 575-83]

For its sheer compression of powerful images, Satan's vir-
tuoso exploitation of pastoral resources exceeds any pastoral
poem I know. His description of the Tree appeals rapidly,
relentlessly, ruthlessly to all five senses, with the last line linking, by means of the caesura, an intense allurement to a wholly innocent image of "play." For the poet and the reader, if
not for Eve, Satan's fatally seductive language indicates a
truth that we saw to be a major preoccupation in Spenser's
pastorals: both language and the senses, for all their beauty,
are corruptible media, frail, and ever to be safeguarded.

Again, it is Satan, not Milton, who abuses the resources of
pastoral. Throughout his career Milton detaches his poet-
speakers from the corruptibility of the natural world in a way
that Spenser never allows Colin Clout to do. The neoplatonic
*scala* provided Colin with the imaginative means of reconcil-
ing the flesh to the spirit: indeed Rosalind's bodily beauty, as
he painfully learns, manifests the beauty of her spirit. Even
though Colin ascended to a visionary moment in "some
cellestiall rage of loue," he never abandoned his fleshly com-
mitments. Milton's pastorals, too, reveal a vertical imaginative design that accounts for the place of the poet in the
universal plan. And like the imaginative design of Spenser's
pastorals, the Miltonic design is literally—that is,
geographically, cosmically, structurally, emotionally,
—spatial.    Of course, to assert that Milton's imagination is spatially oriented will surprise nobody. But where he
employs pastoral, especially in the early poems, Milton's
spatial imagination conceives of the poetic vocation in a
distinct and remarkable way; he consistently portrays the
poet in the central position of a vast universal triad. Rather
than the continuous, ascending ladder by which Colin climbs
to his vision of love, a cosmic triad emerges in Milton's

pastorals, whereby the poet finds himself in the medial and mediating position between the segregated realms of nature and divinity.

This middle terrain of the Miltonic imagination, soaring above human mortality and history and reaching toward divinity, reflects the well-known belief, born in the classical image of man fostered through the Renaissance, that humanity occupies a medial position in the harmonious vertical structure of the universe. This belief has special application to Milton, who attributes such singular power to his own divinely inspired imagination. Between the realms of heaven and fallen nature stands the inspired poet, his robes and garlands flowing about him, in an imaginative realm distinct unto itself, but with allegiances to both the world of created nature and to nature's Creator. These three interlocking but distinct realms or "orders" take shape in the following way in Milton's poetry.[12] The first and basest is the order of nature: the elements, the things of the earth. This order we find portrayed lucidly in terms of pastoral poetry. The second, mediating order is represented by music, as we find it in several forms throughout Milton's canon: the "song" of the poet, the music of the heavenly choirs, the inaudible harmony of the spheres. The third and highest order is divinity, symbolized, as all readers of Milton know, by light.

This universal triadic design reflects the structure of Milton's imagination consistently over a lifetime. In the invocations of *Paradise Lost*, for example, the epic poet gives this design clear and passionate expression.[13] As he begins his account of heaven in book 3, the narrator intones his prayer, "Hail, holy light, ofspring of Heav'n first-born," the "Bright effluence of bright essence increate." Aware of his own mortal imperfection, however, the blind narrator hesitates to "express" God's perfection. He knows, on the other hand, that with "other notes then to th' *Orphean* Lyre" he has been "Taught by the heav'nly Muse to venture down/ The dark descent, and up to reascend," hoping now to equal in renown the "Prophets old" (3.1-36). The means of his vision will be his "sacred Song":

> Then feed on thoughts, that voluntarie move
> Harmonious numbers; as the wakeful Bird
> Sings darkling, and in shadiest Covert hid
> Tunes her nocturnal Note.
>
> [3. 37-40]

The poet's song, following the "Voice divine" (7. 2) of his heavenly Muse, joins in the "Harmonious numbers" that praise the Creator. By this "Celestial Song" he is "[u]p led . . . Into the Heav'n of Heav'ns" and "with like safetie guided down" to his "Native Element" (7. 12-16). And he depicts his natural home, the lowest order, in the beautiful lament for his lost sight, relying explicitly on the imagery of pastoral:

> . . . Thus with the Year
> Seasons return, but not to me returns
> Day, or the sweet approach of Ev'n or Morn,
> Or sight of vernal bloom, or Summers Rose,
> Or flocks, or heards, or human face divine.
>
> [3. 40-44]

The melancholy simplicity of the poet's personal sense of loss should not obscure the profounder implication behind his words. His physical blindness prefigures the inexorable blindness that the "Seasons return" must finally bring to all men. His natural affliction has blessed him with the knowledge that the beauties of natural life must be transcended: "So much the rather thou Celestial light/ Shine inward," he concludes; for with the loveliness of "Natures works . . . expung'd and ras'd," the poet "may see and tell/ Of things invisible to mortal sight" (3. 48-55).

The universal triadic design that the invocations to *Paradise Lost* fully embody certainly did not find such concentration at every stage of Milton's long search for his great subject, but the consistency of the design is remarkable in view of the length and vagaries of his career. It is possible, given what we know of Milton's fervent efforts to unite classical and Christian ideals, that the myth of Orpheus assisted in the evolution of this triadic imaginative universe. In his allusions to Orpheus in the Sixth Elegy, *Ad Patrem*, and the Seventh Prolusion, the young poet doubtless apprehends a strong bond between the powers of the Thracian bard and his own developing sense of his divinely sanctioned mission.[14] We have seen how Spenser frequently alluded to Orpheus in the various roles of lover, primordial pastoral poet, and, at the end of *Colin Clout*, oracular prophet. All of these incarnations of Orpheus helped to focus on Colin's progress as a poet-lover. Milton employs an even greater variety of allusions to Orpheus, most notably when he recalls the violent death of the Thracian at the hands of the crazed Maenads. Whichever aspect of this pliable myth Milton chooses, for whichever thematic reason, it seems safe to say that Orpheus exercises a dual charm over the poet. First, Orpheus represents the archetypal pastoral poet-shepherd; second, and more important, Orpheus was also the archetypal primordial singer. The two roles must be distinguished in Milton's poetry, because of the separation that Milton himself enforces between the realm of pastoral and the mediating power of song. As John Hollander has fully documented, Orpheus's pastoral functions developed side by side in the Renaissance with his importance as a divine musician: "without the civilizing influence of the Orphean music, humanity lapses into barbarism. It takes little straining of analogy for us to see how, *mutatis mutandis*, this purely civil effect may be seen as Christian grace, saving rather than civilizing."[15]

Milton's perception of Orpheus as the mythic patron of pastoral fuses discreetly in the early poems with his attraction to Orpheus the divinely inspired singer. The union of the two mythopoeic roles perhaps accounts for the power that Orpheus claims over Milton's imagination, even until his last, discouraged reference to the singer in book 7 of *Paradise Lost*; it certainly helps account for the creation of an identifiably orphic figure early in Milton's career, the Genius of the Wood.

Probably composed between 1630 and 1634, *Arcades* is announced in the 1645 volume as "Part of an Entertainment," an elaborate encomium to the Countess Dowager of Derby, and therefore the kind of verse that would hardly seem characteristic of a poet dedicated to the pursuit of immortal wisdom. In fact, though, the poem securely represents its author and provides a classic example of Coleridge's famous dictum that Milton "attracts all forms and things to himself, into the unity of his own ideal."[16] The Genius of the Wood speaks with all the power and inspiration of Milton's other poetic spokesmen, and does so, furthermore, in an imaginative domain that suggests the Orpheus of both pastoral and divine song. It is no coincidence, then, that his long speech, which is framed on two sides by the "Songs" of the poem, corresponds to the intermediary position he inhabits between the mortal and divine realms of Milton's triadic universe.

As a masque *Arcades* relies on the stately effect created by the procession of shepherds to the presence of the "rural Queen," the splendor of whom even "All *Arcadia* hath not seen" (95). The first song finds her

> Sitting like a Goddes bright,
> In the center of her light,
>
> [19-20]

amidst all the "blaze of Majesty" (2) that we associate with Milton's refulgent light imagery to express the "unexpressive." She is, as the shepherds say, "Too divine to be mistook" (4). Before they can approach her, though, the

Genius appears before them and offers "with all helpful service" to "lead" them on their "quest" (34-40).

In his monologue the Genius justifies himself as their proper guide to the presence of the rural Queen by explaining not only his duties as caretaker of the pastoral landscape but also the source of his authority over it:

> For know by lot from *Jove* I am the powr
> Of this fair Wood, and live in Oak'n bowr
> To nurse the Saplings tall, and curl the grove
> With Ringlets quaint; and wanton windings wove.
> And all my Plants I save from nightly ill
> Of noisom winds, and blasting vapours chill.
>
> [44-49]

The Genius's vigilance over the landscape, which could otherwise fall prey to all the evils of chaotic natural life, typifies the orphic pastoral poet gifted "by lot from *Jove*." His "puissant words, and murmurs made to bless" (60) echo those of the Thracian patron of innumerable pastoral poems.

His duties as the guardian of the landscape allow him another privilege, one that augments his authority by associating him with Orpheus the poet-musician:

> . . . when drowsines
> Hath lock't up mortal sense, then listen I
> To the celestial *Sirens* harmony,
> That sit upon the nine enfolded Sphears . . .
> And keep unsteddy Nature to her law,
> And the low world in measur'd motion draw
> After the heavenly tune, which none can hear
> Of human mould with gross unpurged ear.
>
> [61-74]

The music of the spheres, to which the Genius has special access, doubtless aids and perhaps even inspires him, in the realm of his own landscape, to "keep unsteddy Nature to her law." His attunement to these celestial harmonies, a privilege not granted to those of "human mould with gross unpurged ear," also bestows upon him a power of expression that makes him worthy to lead the shepherds in their quest. Many of Milton's commentators have documented his lifelong fascination with Platonic-Pythagorean theories of the music of the spheres, and, as everyone knows, music in its varying forms represents for Milton the harmony and order of the universe.[17] In the Genius's speech, Milton's most explicit poetic exposition of Plato's version of the inaudible music of the spheres from book 10 of *The Republic*, we see that the Genius's ministrations to the landscape are predicated upon his ability, as it is expressed in "At a Solemn Music," to "keep in tune with Heav'n" (26). Moreover, the Genius's own song, by which he will lead the Arcadian shepherds to the rural Queen, derives its energy from the heavenly harmonies. He admits that his own "inferior hand or voice" (77) is not worthy of her "peerles height" (75); nonetheless, his powers, "what ere the skill of lesser gods can show," will attend the pilgrims "to her glittering state" (79-82).

As the inheritor of Orpheus the pastoral poet and Orpheus the divine musician, the Genius stands midway between the pastoral "low world" of "mortal sense" and the "blaze of majesty," the "radiant state" of the rural Queen. Milton's patterning of the imagery in the poem is enriched by the dual evocation of the Orpheus myth. By virtue of his uniquely intermediary position in the triadic design of the poem's universe, the Genius may justly exhort the shepherds to

> Follow me as I sing
> And touch the warbled string . . .
> Follow me,
> I will bring you where she sits
> Clad in splendor as befits
> Her deity.
>
> [86-93]

The Genius of *Arcades* assumes greater distinction if we

consider him an avatar of Milton's speaker in a far richer poem, "On the Morning of Christ's Nativity." The ode displays a multiplicity of styles and conventions, and a wide range of reference—not only temporal and spatial, but also literary—in order to focus on a paramount event in Christian history. All of the impressive virtues that have stimulated numerous critics of the ode doubtless also prompted Milton to place it at the beginning of the English poems in the 1645 volume and to append to its title the informative words "Compos'd 1629." That Milton invites us to examine his talents on the eve of his twenty-first birthday in the light of the poem's heritage, stretching back to Pindar and Virgil's fourth *Eclogue*, alerts us to the assertion the ode will make about its poet's developing vocation. In the course of the poem this assertion evolves according to a design similar to the triadic universe that *Arcades* captures within a relatively uncomplicated compass. The ode therefore incorporates within its variety of styles, allusions, and conventions those of pastoral in a special way. By tapping the resources of pastoral and by inviting us to compare his ode to Virgil's messianic *Eclogue*, Milton announces his divinely endowed spokesman as the Christian *vates* of pastoral poetry, capable of bringing heaven to earth.

Milton found in Virgil's messianic *Eclogue* more than a lofty subject, worthy of imitation, that is, the celebration of a child whose birth heralds a new golden age.[18] He also found in Virgil's poem an affinity for the Arcadian poet who narrates the *Eclogue*. In his opening words (*paulo maiora canamus*) he announces that his song will far surpass the humble decorum of pastoral. Accordingly, then, his invocation to the Sicilian Muses abjures conventional supplication in favor of forthright self-assertiveness: "Muses of Sicily, let us attempt a rather more exalted theme." He continues to subvert pastoral humility by voicing the wish that the landscape be worthy of his song. His acceptance of the pastoral mode, then, if not grudging, is at least partly ironic:

Si canimus silvas, silvae sunt consule dignae.

[3]

If we must sing of woodlands, let them be such as may do a Consul honour.

The Arcadian poet's sense of his prophetic role sustains him throughout his catalogue of the blessings that the new age will bring to nature and man. At the conclusion of the poem, he boldly assumes center stage again, with a final prophecy of what his own achievements will encompass, if he could be allowed to chronicle the events of the impending golden age:

non me carminibus vincat nec Thracius Orpheus,
nec Linus, mater quamvis atque huic pater adsit,
Orphei Calliopea, Lino formosus Apollo.

[55-57]

Then neither Thracian Orpheus nor Linus could outsing me, not though the one had his mother and the other had his father at his side, Orpheus, his Calliope, and Linus, Apollo in all his beauty.

The proem to Milton's ode shares with Virgil's *Eclogue* a similar disposition toward the poetic feat that is being performed, an attitude that calls as much attention to the verbal act as it does to the subject it celebrates. Milton's speaker goes to no small effort to ensure that the attention of his audience is fixed upon his own performance as well as upon the sacred mystery he is about to commemorate. Numerous critics have noticed how Milton's use of tenses and time in the ode contributes to the "simultaneity of all moments under the aspect of eternity."[19] Indeed, the first line, "This is the Month, and this the happy morn," draws our attention to the poet who celebrates this happy event. With his wondrous range of vision, he himself stands in the present tense, as it were, of the Nativity, midway between the Creation and the final day when "at last our bliss/ Full and perfet is" (165-66).

As the proem unfolds, he augments his authority by establishing his rightful place in a long line of poet-prophets; but instead of Virgil's Orpheus and Linus, the singer of the ode remembers that the "holy Sages once did sing" (5) of the Messiah's advent that he will now celebrate. His Muse therefore is a "Heav'nly Muse," who has placed at the poet's disposal a "sacred vein" (15). Like Virgil, he wastes no words in supplication to this heavenly Muse, but commands her to "run" with her ode, to "lay it lowly at his blessed feet" (24-25). It is important not to underestimate the value of Milton's employment of the stock figure of the Muse in the ode. In her well-known essay on the poem, Rosemond Tuve emphasizes that Milton's use of this traditional figure "is no tag of adornment, but a necessary help to say what he could of himself have no offering to bring." The Muse brings, as Tuve seems to have been the first to perceive, a gift in the form of an act of praise; furthermore, "a hymn is not only a 'praise,' but usually a liturgical act of praise, by definition usually written as Sidney says '*to imitate the inconceivable excellencies of God.*' "[20]

And so the speaker in the proem reconciles two quite opposing attitudes toward his task at hand. He imputes his praise to a "Heav'nly Muse," a source of inspiration in some sense superior to him and whose help he requires in his "liturgical act of praise." At the same time, he addresses this Muse imperatively, even magisterially: "See . . .run . . . lay it lowly . . . joyn thy voice." The last lines of the proem capture his dual attitude by means of a discreet, syntactic ambiguity:

> And joyn thy voice unto the Angel Quire,
> From out his secret Altar toucht with hallow'd fire.
> [27-28]

From its position in the line it would seem that the "Hallow'd fire" could be touching: (1) the Lord's altar (which makes nonsense of the image); (2) the "Angel Quire"; or (3) the voice of the Muse. But because we know that the poet clearly alludes to the hallowing coal that purged the lips of Isaiah, we sense that the poet himself (and perhaps also the Muse and the choir) has been touched with fire of the Lord. Without overtly intruding upon the scene, the poet nonetheless closes the proem with an allusion that directs our attention back to his own divinely inspired powers.

The proem establishes, then, the significance of the poet's "liturgical act of praise." In doing so, it also develops in its imagery the universal triadic design that the hymn will give life to. In the second stanza of the proem, the poet depicts a vast cosmic scene that distinctly segregates heaven from earth, a scene that the poet's song, in the form of the hymn, will attempt to reconcile:

> That glorious Form, that Light unsufferable,
> And that far-beaming blaze of Majesty
> Wherewith he wont at Heav'ns high Councel-Table,
> To sit the midst of Trinal Unity,
> He laid aside; and here with us to be,
>     Forsook the Courts of everlasting Day,
> And chose with us a darksom House of mortal Clay.
>                                                  [8-14]

The "Trinal Unity" of "Light unsufferable" has been broken, forsaken so that the "Son of Heav'ns eternal king" (2) may descend to our fallen "darksom House of mortal Clay." Having defined this radical gap between heaven and earth, the poet then turns to his Muse, asking if she has "no verse, no hymn, no solemn strein" (17) to welcome the "approaching light" (20) of divinity come to earth. Here the Muse's song anticipates the light of both the "Suns team" (19) and the "spangled host" of "squadrons bright" (21), the light, that is, of both nature and divinity. The next stanza reinforces this special relationship between "song" and "light." The song of the Muse anticipates light: "O run, prevent [the Star-led Wisards] with thy humble ode" (24). At the same time, the Muse's song deserves a place among the heavenly harmonies: "And joyn thy voice unto the Angel Quire" (27). The Muse's song—and, by extension, the poet's gift—are inferior to, but simultaneously point toward, the manifestations of divinity, represented, of course, by light.

But what, we may ask, of that "darksom House of mortal Clay," man's life in nature, that the poet briefly mentioned in his subtle proem? As the hymn begins, the speaker focuses on the Natvitiy's *mise-en-scène*, the earth and its phenomena. Some years ago Arthur Barker elucidated the ode according to its three movements. I hasten to note now that his explanation of the poem's technical structure is not the same as the imaginative, universal design that I see embodied in the poem. His analysis has proved just and useful, however, and at the risk of confusion I must rehearse it here. The first eight stanzas of the hymn, Barker notes, describe the setting of the Nativity; the next nine, the angelic choir and the music of the spheres; the last nine, the flight of the heathen gods.[21] In the proem, we have seen suggested a relationship between the mediating song of the Muse and the approaching light of divinity. In the hymn, that suggestion is amplified in the appropriately central stanzas (9-16), because, as the poet says, "such harmony alone/ Could hold all Heav'n and Earth in happier union." Meanwhile, the first movement of the hymn depicts our dark and fallen home, culminating in the pastoral vignette of stanza 8.

Milton again may have had Virgil's fourth *Eclogue* directly in mind for the description of nature in the first movement of the hymn; after all, Virgil's enumeration of the benefits induced by nature's return to the golden age became an essential feature of the messianic poem thereafter.[22] Milton responds to the pressures of the convention that called for the transformation of nature in a characteristically unconventional way. Rather than a literal rendition in the Virgilian manner of nature's luxurious metamorphosis (the very cradle

of Virgil's child is adorned with flowers: *ipsa tibi blandos
fundent cunabala flores* [23]), Milton employs a lavish series
of artificial conceits that suggest by means of prosopopeia the
universal alteration of nature. The stars "stand fixt in sted-
fast gaze" (70); the sun "hid his head for shame" (80); nature
"doff't her gawdy trim" (33); the ocean "quite forgot to rave"
(67). By conforming to the conventions of the tradition
almost with a vengeance, Milton calls into scrutiny that very
tradition. At the same time, he portrays the natural processes
as temporarily halted from participating in what can only be
regarded as their normally sinister activities. The same
enslavement to sin that subjugates man enthrals all created
nature; with man was ruined his natural home. Nature, therefore, wearing a "gawdy trim," is accustomed to "wanton with
the Sun her lusty Paramour" (36). The blatant sensuality of the
personifications, like Satan's exploitation of pastoral imagery
to ruin Eve, insinuates the unhappy corruption inherent in
fallen life. Nature's attempt to conceal this, to "hide her guilty front" with a "Saintly Vail of Maiden white" snow, only
accentuates her "sinfull blame" and "foul deformities"
(39-44). Man himself and all his wretched works, his "spear
and shield," his "hooked Chariot" (55-56), participate in the
general woe that Christ has come to redeem.

The last stanza of the first movement, drawing on the
gospel narrative, unmistakably relies on pastoral resources:

> The Shepherds on the Lawn,
> Or ere the point of dawn,
>    Sat simply chatting in a rustick row;
> Full little thought they than
> That the mighty *Pan*
>    Was kindly come to live with them below;
> Perhaps their loves, or else their sheep,
> Was all that did their silly thoughts so busie keep.
>
> [85-92]

Miss Tuve justly calls this stanza an "*icon*," observing that "for the first time in his poem Milton wants us to be present, in our bodies, at an event. Immediacy to the senses is the dictating aim of *icon*."[23] This immediacy, it may be added, accentuates the speaker's ironic reference to the "mighty *Pan*." The simple swains are unaware of the astral changes that have been taking place above them, and they cling—like pastoral poetry itself—to their "silly thoughts" of false rural deities, the dryads and Pan of a darker age. The shepherds have been rendered insensible by the very fact of their mortal condition; a sound nothing less than heavenly must awaken them:

> When such musick sweet
> Their hearts and ears did greet,
>   As never was by mortal finger strook,
> Divinely warbl'd voice
> Answering the stringed noise,
>   As all their souls in blissful rapture took.
>
> [93-98]

The divine music that reverberates in the shepherds' fallen "hearts and ears" affords them a blissful rapture unknown since "the sons of morning sung" (119) at the Creation. These harmonious sounds, which Barker identifies as dominating the second movement of the poem (9-16), have rightly received much critical attention.[24] Announcing a change in human history, the angelic harmony that intrudes upon the shepherds' quiet suggests to the poet similar inaudible melodies that he fervently details in one joyous stanza after another. The angelic symphony recalls the primordial hymns sung "While the Creator Great/ His Constellations set" (120-21); this in turn summons up the Pythogorean-Platonic music of the "Crystall sphears" (125). At the end of his ecstasy, the poet cries out for all the harmonies to continue,

> For if such holy Song
> Enwrap our fancy long,

Time will run back and fetch the age of gold.
[133-135]

His wish, of course, is conditional; the pastoral age of gold
has long vanished, and innocence cannot be restored until the
"wakefull trump of doom" (156) has ended history and announced eternity. Nevertheless, the poet has glimpsed, in the
midst of his rhapsodic description of celestial harmony, a vision of the final day when Heaven will "open wide the Gates
of her high Palace Hall" (148). And that vision, mediated by
music, is drawn in terms of light.[25] In fact, throughout his
catalogue of the potential effects of divine harmony, the poet
has faithfully adhered to the triadic design forecast in the
proem. The divine harmonies, as ravishing as they are, only
anticipate a more exalted experience, when "Hell it self shall
pass away/ And leave her dolorous mansions to the peering
day" (139-40). Similarly, the shepherds are *first* enraptured
by the "thousand echo's" of "each heav'nly close" (100);
only *thereafter* are they receptive to the highest bliss:

At last surrounds their sight
A Globe of circular light,
    That with long beams the shame-fac't night array'd
The helmed Cherubim
And sworded Seraphim,
    Are seen in glittering ranks with wings displaid,
Harping in loud and solemn quire,
With unexpressive notes to Heav'ns new-born Heir.
[109-16]

Music—even the unexpressive notes of the harping angelic
choir—only prefigures the vision of "A Globe of circular
light" (can there be found an image more expressive of
Milton's vision of perfection?). Just as the song of the Muse
in the proem "prevent[ed]" (came before) the approaching
light, so here the "holy Song" of the spheres and angels yield
before the "peering day" of eternal joy. Relying on the im-

petus of music/poetry as a mediating power between the realms of nature and divinity, the hymn maintains the triadic, vertical pattern promised in the proem. It follows, therefore, that the poet conceives his ultimate vision of eternity solely in terms of light (stanza 16). At the end of time, the "Trinal Unity" that had been disrupted by Christ's descent to earth will reappear in the form of the trinity of Truth and Justice, clad in rainbows; and

Mercy will sit between,
Thron'd in Celestial sheen,
With radiant feet the tissued clouds down stearing.
[144-46]

The poet's final vision of course cannot mark the end of the poem: "But wisest Fate sayes no" (149). The Day of Judgment must be preceded by the slow pace of history. The third movement of the ode, which describes the rout of the pagan gods, continues to perplex and delight many readers, not least because it raises the fundamental question of its very inclusion in a poem celebrating the incarnation.[26] While a number of suggestions have been made from biographical, theological, stylistic, and generic perspectives to explain Milton's emphasis on the pagan gods, it may prove useful to consider this section of the poem from a pastoral perspective. Amid the "shadows dread" (206) and "scaly Horrour" (172) of the rout there is one stanza that stands out by virtue of its relative gentleness:

The lonely mountains o're,
And the resounding shore,
   A voice of weeping heard, and loud lament;
From haunted spring, and dale
Edg'd with poplar pale,
   The parting Genius is with sighing sent,
With flowre-inwov'n tresses torn
The Nimphs in twilight shade of tangled thickets mourn.
[181-88]

More than elsewhere in the poem, we hear an almost melancholy note of regret from the poet over the departure of what man has found beautiful in his natural home.[27] The Genius that has brought the beauties of the landscape closer to men must be "with sighing sent"; the shore resounds with weeping for the "flowre-inwov'n tresses torn." We may choose perhaps to hear in this stanza a softening of the poet's description of corrupted nature in the early stanzas of the hymn, almost as a compensatory recognition of the genuine beauty of nature and the pastoral poetry that has so long expressed it. Whatever loveliness the natural world holds, though, must be adjusted by a higher wisdom. The hollow shrieks and "hideous humm" (174) of the pagan deities pervade the landscape and must be silenced by the triumphant "bliss" that "now begins" (165-67). As a symbol of what is fallen, pastoral and the order of nature must be transcended.

Hence the final stanza of the ode returns to the two higher orders, leaving the order of nature behind. The poet refers one last time to the order of music: "Time is our tedious Song should here have ending."[28] The "holy Song" of the angelic chorus as well as the "solemn strein" of the Muse have symbolically joined, or perhaps inspired, the poet's song, his only direct mention of the ode as *his* song. And just as both of those earlier songs possess only a limited power, a mediating power that leads to a higher vision of "light," so too the poet's song—"tedious" because inferior to the ravishing heavenly song—leads to the vision ("But see") in the final stanza. Both heaven and Bethlehem are now robed in light:

> Heav'ns youngest teemed Star,
> Hath fixt her polisht Car,
>   Her sleeping Lord with Handmaid Lamp attending:
> And all about the Courtly Stable
> Bright-harnest Angels sit in order serviceable.
>
>                                    [240-44]

Music, the mediating poetic agent of universal order, has now been refined away, leaving the purity of "Bright-harnest Angels."

Milton concludes the ode, as he began it, by calling attention to the poet's accomplishment; and in this respect again, he may have taken his cue from Virgil's messianic poem. Both poets find themselves in a peculiarly solitary position with respect to the "world" that their poems embody. For Virgil, all through the *Eclogues*, solitude seems to precondition lofty poetic achievement; when the Arcadian poet steps before us, he presents himself as the only living man able to carry the weight of the tradition that has descended to him from ancient days.[29] At these moments Virgil plainly anticipates the young Milton. His early poems distinguish themselves as the issue of Milton's pen by their character as solitary mediations. This familiar Miltonic hallmark, culminating in the great blind bard of the epic, takes on special significance in those poems where we find the poet alone in a landscape. Perhaps this special solitude, perfectly suited to a poet convinced of his calling as a divinely inspired *vates*, recommended the Orpheus myth to him so strongly. In any event, it is helpful to compare briefly Milton's emphasis on poetic solitude to Spenser's treatment of this theme in his pastorals.

Spenser fills his pastoral scenes with characters, many of whom have names and qualities approaching those of fictional characters (such as Hobbinol). The *Calender* and *Colin Clout* portray communities of rustic figures, exercising various social relations. Far from being a desirable condition, solitude for Colin proves to be highly destructive of his talents. At his nadir, Colin "in the desert chose to dwell," isolated from the company of friends for whose benefit he ought to have been practicing his ennobling skill. His lovelorn retreat signaled not only the self-destructive effects of his inability to deal with his natural lot, but also his abnegation of his poetic responsibilities. Only after he has returned to his proper bucolic community can he effectively exercise his powers for the delight and instruction of his peers.

Milton's poets have no peers. We see reflected in his solitary speakers the centripetal energies that Coleridge's famous remark attributes to Milton's genius: his singular personae bear unmistakable affinities to their brooding private creator. Even the Genius of the Wood, whose epiphany in a social situation would seem to demand some sort of integration into the life of society, stands, by virtue of his unique relation to the landscape and his attunement to the inaudible spheric harmony, in unusual and highly privileged solitude. Pastoral solitude, far from being invidious, predicates successful utterance in Milton's pastoral meditations.

It is with these observations in mind that we may best approach the "twin" poems *L'Allegro-Il Penseroso*, where Milton returns to the meditative vein of the ode and provides one of the best-known portraits of Milton the young poet grappling with the choices that lie before him. Keats's fondness for the companion poems reminds us of their peculiarly subjective character, and indeed we often sense that these poems are enunciated directly out of the poet's imagination. As L'Allegro and Il Penseroso move each through his ideal day, defining his own relationship to what he observes around him, each one provides an important instance of the Renaissance truism which established a correspondence between the inner world of man and the shape of the outer cosmos. Each poem presents a natural "world," a microcosm delineated by the poet's imagination. Milton's characteristic attempt to encompass the entire universe within a poem, an attempt already realized in the Ode, is newly affirmed in *L'Allegro-Il Penseroso*. Glancing from heaven to earth, from earth to heaven, the companion poems share with the ode an expansive imaginative terrain that is mapped on a similar, albeit less sharply defined, triadic cosmic pattern.

Yet the world of the twin poems seems far removed from the Christmas eve of the ode. In the twin poems we witness no event of overarching significance. We hear no prophetic voice edifying an experience that affects all the sons of Adam. No chorus of angels breaks through quotidian routines to herald a momentous shift in history. We have instead, at least at first glance, an entertaining, ingeniously constructed diptych portraying complementary modes of experience. The "day" of the cheerful man is balanced, and indeed necessary to, the contemplative "night" of the pensive man. We follow each in succession through his round of sheltered leisure, compare the pleasures of each life-style; and even if we no longer conclude that these are the "ponderous trifles" that critics once took them to be, we often search in vain for the great argument of the later epic bard.[30] In the last thirty years commentators have taken the poems more seriously, exploring the imagery, allusions, and background, and have succeeded in establishing them firmly as worthy of the Miltonic canon. Yet the poems still may seem slightly off center, slightly off the main course of justifying the ways of God to men, and still, after all, only an "exercise" in the poet's search to find a surer role for his genius. *L'Allegro-Il Penseroso* lie, in fact, within the boundaries of Milton's imaginative course and are a secure and logical poetic outcome of the ode. Together they constitute an important statement about pastoral and Milton's growing ideas about pastoral as a mode of experience, ideas that will take definitive shape in *Lycidas*.

The prophet's role assumed in the ode does not figure strongly in the twin poems, because such a role would be inappropriate to a situation that lacks the earlier poem's sweep. The twin poems do not soar above history and time; they have a local habitation and a name. At the end of *Il Penseroso*, however, the pensive man looks forward to that loftier role again, and he enjoins Melancholy to bless him one day with her ultimate "pleasure," the attainment of "something like Prophetic strain" (174). In the twin poems, then, the two speakers can be said (with only a slight straining at paradox) to prefigure the vocational and emotional process that must have motivated the bardic singer of the earlier ode. Milton enacts this process, which is nothing less than the process of the imagination, by placing each speaker in the midst of the natural world. This positioning is accomplished structurally in much the same way as in the Ode. In that poem the middle stanzas (9-14) consisted of the speaker's joyous description of the heavenly harmonies, a description, it will be remembered, that had explicit metaphoric connections with the poet's faith in the efficacy of his own art. The middle stanzas of the ode, then, reflected schematically the role of the poet-prophet in the grand design of the universe.

A similar design prevails in *L'Allegro-Il Penseroso*. Each poem is divided into five thematic units after the induction. The third and therefore central unit in each poem most clearly captures the dilemma of its speaker and defines his unique relationship to the universe. Also, of course, these central lines help to define the relationship of the cheerful man to the pensive man, and in so doing, become the keystones in two carefully conceived and constructed imaginative arches. In *L'Allegro* the central lines (69-99) find the cheerful man turning from the pleasures of the sunrise and entering into a "measure[ment]" (70) and description of the landscape around him. He accomplishes this primarily in pastoral terms. In *Il Penseroso* the central lines (77-96) begin as the pensive man moves from the night air to within doors, where he undertakes his own solitary measurement, the observance of the heavenly spheres, accompanied by the music of the cricket and "the Belman's drowsie charm" (83). This section of the poem, the quiet counterpart of the central section of *L'Allegro*, is rendered with reference to astronomy and philosophy. A juxtaposition of the two central passages suggests the progress of the two poems taken together as one: we pass from *L'Allegro* to *Il Penseroso* with a corresponding shift in vision, as it were, from the beauties of the landscape to the beauties of the heavenly realm. Structurally, as well as thematically, *L'Allegro* heralds *Il Penseroso* and provides the necessary pleasures that are superceded by the higher and more profound pleasures of *Il Penseroso*.[31]

The inductions to each poem have been characterized both as "burlesques," that is, as parodies of academic verse, and as banishments of the travesty of what is praised in the companion poem.[32] In either case, each induction with its overwrought histrionics signals an initiation into a highly artificial world, thick with literary allusion. This is especially true of *L'Allegro*, less so of *Il Penseroso*, where the literary tone has been previously established. In the first poem Melancholy, a creature of the classical underworld, born of Cerberus "in *Stygian* Cave forlorn" (3), is banished to yet another literary land, the Cimmerian desert. The point is important for what is to follow in *L'Allegro*. The allusions in the poem are pervasively pagan, and given what we know of Milton's lifelong concern with the union of classical and Christian, it notably lacks the redemptive auspices of the Christian promise. In itself this emphasis carries no moral burden; but the situation is analogous to Milton's later allusions to the pagan earthly gardens in *Paradise Lost*: the existence of Eden causes them, for all their glory, to wither by comparison. In the same way, *L'Allegro* pales and its exuberant paganism assumes a less charmed significance when placed in retrospect against *Il Penseroso*.

Classical allusions are heavily deployed in the first of *L'Allegro*'s five sections (11-40). These lines are devoted to an invocation of Mirth, an account of her genesis and a catalogue of her attributes. The speaker suggests that she was sired by Bacchus on Venus, or alternatively, that she was conceived on beds of violets by Zephyr and the playful Aurora. In either event her origins suggest her erotic potentiality. This "bucksom, blith, and debonair" (24) figure possesses a sensuality accentuated by her attendants, those personifications of the drawing room, "wanton Wiles,/ Nods, and Becks, and Wreathed Smiles" (27-28). The "dimple sleek" (30) in which her attendants love to live enhances her undeniable charm.

This catalogue suggests no, or hardly any, moral censure, and the speaker expresses only a lusty exuberance in the aura of Mirth's anticipated arrival. L'Allegro wants to be admitted to her crew, to join "the Mountain Nymph, sweet Liberty" (36) and to pass "unreproved" (40) through the pastoral delights she can offer him.

The second section of the poem (41-68), beginning with the ascent of the lark, still anticipates the fullest pleasures that Mirth affords, and brings the cheerful man to a thrice-told description of the dawn. He hears the lark singing and witnesses the sunrise "through the Sweet-Briar, or the Vine,/ Or the twisted Eglantine" (47-48) of his rural bower. The cock, meanwhile, "stoutly struts his Dames before" (52), thus echoing the sexual element abumbrated in the first section of the poem. Both sound and light seem to act in concord in these lines. While the sun performs its pageant "[r]oab'd in flames" (61), the plowman whistles, the milkmaid sings, and every shepherd tells his tale. The cheerful man, however, has no part in all these activities other than that of the detached observer. This point has been made often, but it needs stressing.³³ He sees the masque-like ceremony of the sun in state, he hears the echoing sounds of hound and horn, he observes the rural characters of the landscape before him. But his place in the scene in undefined or indefinite. His passivity, here only suggested, later in *L'Allegro* solidified, and in contrast to the pensive man irrefutable, emerges as L'Allegro's primary attribute.

This observation is confirmed in the third and central section of the poem (66-69), where L'Allegro begins his description of the landscape:

Streit mine eye hath caught new pleasures
Whilst the Lantskip round it measures,
Russet Lawns, and Fallows Gray,
Where the nibling flocks do stray,
Mountains on whose barren brest

The labouring clouds do often rest
Meadows trim with Daisies pide,
Shallow Brooks, and Rivers wide.

[69-76]

This passage could have been taken from Thomson and War-
ton. The rhyming couplets and balanced sound effects, accentuated by the repetition of "do" to fill out the meter, give
the verse a startlingly Augustan effect. Felicitously organized, calm, and consonant with L'Allegro's sense of well-being,
both the diction and the landscape reflect a static habit of
mind. Like Donne's sleeping lover, sucking on country
pleasures, he remains unaware and unmeditative. This is not
to say that he, or the landscape, partakes of any sinful or corrupt activity. But he is—to put it bluntly—empty and asleep,
as *Il Penseroso*, by way of instructive contrast, will make
clear. The conventional pastoral domesticity that he next
records enhances, indeed prettifies, the essential sterility of
his situation. Corydon and Thyrsis eat their "Country
Messes" prepared by the "neat-handed" Phillis (85-86). The
vignette is charming. It marks the poem's turn to English
folklore, English paganism, at the same time that it
strengthens L'Allegro's exclusion from rural society. We
have no sense that the cheerful man belongs even peripherally
to the pastoral delights he records with such finesse. Perhaps
this is why the central lines provide such a strong sense of
order and harmony. Not only the balanced phrasing, but also
the symmetrical patterns that the cheerful man observes in
the landscape support the tranquil orderliness that constitutes
the crux of his poem. Clouds seem to rest on top of mountains, while battlements are "boosom'd" (78) in trees; the
cottage chimney smokes between two oaks, and Phillis
"dresses" (86) the meal with as sure a hand as she "binds"
(88) the sheaves. Not until we learn what occupies Il
Penseroso in the later poem's corresponding lines (78-96),
where, instead of carefully arranged landscapes, we participate in the unfolding of Plato's spheres, do we have any

cause to impugn L'Allegro's observations nor any reason to
regard the activities of his cheerful day more skeptically than
he himself does.

The fourth section of *L'Allegro* (91-130) concerns the fairy
tales of the country folk and the romances and pageants of
the evening. The Draytonesque and peculiarly English country legends and rural characters that the cheerful man hears
balance the classical tales of Mirth's genesis in the first section of the poem. These details thus share the amoral, sensual
character, whereby maids are pinched and youths dance in
the shade, of the earlier Ovidian romps. This note continues
to echo in the lines about "Towred Cities" (117) where
"Ladies, whose bright eies/ Rain influences," are fought
over in tournaments of high chivalry. Once again, there is
nothing corrupt or culpable here. They are merely

> Such sights as youthful Poets dream
> On Summer eeves by haunted stream
>
> [129-30]

and lack the depth and wisdom that comes with maturity.
L'Allegro's sensibility, like the pagan exuberance that he personifies, is undeveloped and amoral.

The final section (131-50) recapitulates what has preceded
and is almost exclusively concerned with poetry and its effect
on the cheerful man's spirit. The

> . . . lincked sweetness long drawn out,
> With wanton heed, and giddy cunning,
> The melting voice through mazes running,
>
> [140-42]

that Lydian airs married to immortal verse breed in the cheerful man remind us perhaps of Orsino's music, the food of
love, from *Twelfth Night*. Although L'Allegro is not trying
to sicken his appetite, like Orsino, he does want to be nar-
cotized. He wants Mirth to "lap" (136) him in the melting

sounds of the sensual Lydian mode. The "wanton" (141) lux-
uriance of these final lines accords, of course, with the pervasively pagan quality of *L'Allegro* as a whole. But, addi-
tionally, this final section accentuates the shallowness inherent in L'Allegro's values. The cheerful man does nothing
active, even when he is washed over by the ravishing Lydian
harmonies. Hence, the concluding image of Orpheus, noticed
by most commentators on the poem, is precisely appropriate.
Like the cheerful man throughout the poem, Orpheus
"hears" (147) the strains of music passively; he does not actually create and produce those strains himself, as he will in
the corresponding image in *Il Penseroso*.[34] It is significant,
too, that rather than Orpheus's strength as the tamer of
nature or the divine musician, his failure as a poet is stressed:
this music "would have" (148) caused Pluto to relent.[35]

*L'Allegro*'s concluding emphasis on the role of the poet
recalls Milton's use of the triadic design that the twin poems
share with the ode. All three orders of the universe—pastoral,
music, and light—help to structure these poems as well.
Music and light imagery have both received a good share of
critical attention; Kester Svendsen, for example, has traced
the "sound patterns" in the twin poems and has concluded
that L'Allegro hears the music around him without being
strongly moved by its mystery or power.[36] The pensive man,
on the other hand, achieves his vision through the agency of
Christian religious music. He experiences what the speaker of
the ode said could happen when man in some way hears the
holy song of heaven. In a similar way, pastoral is left behind
by the pensive man. There is one early allusion in his poem to
pastoral. In the first section, when he recounts Melancholy's
genesis, he tells us that she was born of Saturn in the golden
age. A contrast between Mirth (born of Venus and Bachus)
and Melancholy is implied, of course; also, the image of
Saturn's reign summons up a more perfect pastoral than that
left behind in *L'Allegro*. On the whole, the method of *Il
Penseroso* calls attention to the differences between the two

speakers. A comparison between them reveals a healthy progression of sensibility from the first to the second poem. Indeed, if the twin poems are read, as they often have been, as debates between two different outlooks on experience, then Il Penseroso would naturally have all the advantages of following one's opponent and being able to refute his arguments point by point.[37] L'Allegro, of course, lacks this opportunity. When in the induction, for example, Il Penseroso banishes Mirth as the "brood of folly without father bred," he alludes deprecatingly to the pagan eroticism that permeated the texture of his opponent's presentation. This tendency applies also the speaker's use of the phrase "idle brain" (5): we think back to the cheerful man's passivity and his insubstantial involvement with his environment. Whereas the induction of the earlier poem, with its classical allusions and literary quality, introduced themes to follow directly in that poem, the induction to Il Penseroso says as much about what preceded it as it does about what is to come. The phrase "fickle Pensioners of Morpheus train" (10), for example, colors in retrospect L'Allegro's self-depiction as the youthful poet dreaming by the haunted stream.

Correspondingly, then, the first section of Il Penseroso (11-55) begins with the line "But hail, thou Goddess, sage and holy." The religious emphasis, if not yet overtly Christian, contrasts with the pagan aura surrounding Mirth. Melancholy is "divinest" (12); her "Saintly visage is too bright/ To hit the Sense of human sight" (13-14); she is "devout and pure" (31). No wanton coupling marked her origin. She was born of the chaste Vesta before carnality became sinful. Peace, Quiet and "Spare Fast" (46), all specifically Christian attributes, are Melancholy's attendants. Milton goes to great lengths to ensure that we understand Melancholy as the companion of order and harmony. Her "eev'n step, and musing gait" (38) are emblematic of the total control that she exercises over experience. The excess and frivolity of Mirth become, if not odious, at least suspect, when placed beside Melancholy's sure-footed steadiness. At the same time, Milton emphasizes Melancholy's importance to the poetic disposition (a theme that will conclude *Il Penseroso*). One of her attendants

> . . . hears the Muses in a ring,
> Aye round about *Joves* Altar sing,
>
> [47-48]

reminding us by means of the dual images of song and circle ("ring . . . sing") of poetry's close association with the Platonic emblems of perfection. In a similar way, Melancholy's "looks commercing with the skies" (39) anticipate Il Penseroso's subsequent enthrallment by the heavenly spheres. Leading him to this surcharged, receptive state of mind by means of her companion, "The Cherub Contemplation" (54), Melancholy will leave the pensive man open to the "extacies" (165), that he foresees at the close of the poem.

The second section of *Il Penseroso* (56-76) begins with the speaker going out to "woo" (64) the nightingale. Whereas L'Allegro sat at home and merely heard the lark, Il Penseroso actively seeks out the "Chauntress" (63). He walks out to behold the moon, while L'Allegro waited inertly for the dawn. Even as he "walks unseen/ On the dry smooth-shaven Green" (65-66), he conveys a mobility that is lacking in the corresponding section of the earlier poem. His physical position on a "Plat of rising round" (73), as the moon "stoop[s]" (12) through the clouds, provides an image by which we may judge Il Penseroso. He almost seems to rise physically upwards in an effort to shorten the distance between heaven and earth.

The central section of the poem (77-96) strengthens this impression, when the pensive man steps within doors and looks to the heavens to "outwatch the *Bear*" (87). His only "resort of mirth" (81) is the music of the cricket and the bellman's "drowsy charm" (83). "Charm" is the key word here. A

hallowed air envelops Il Penseroso's environment, where very
doors are "bless[ed]" (84). He finds himself alone, much as
L'Allegro was in the midst of his pastoral landscape. Instead
of the prettily constructed natural scene of the earlier poem,
though, the view of the heavens open to Il Penseroso lays
bare the very secrets of the universe:

> . . . I may oft outwatch the *Bear*,
> With thrice great *Hermes*, or unsphear
> The spirit of *Plato* to unfold
> What Worlds, or what vast Regions hold
> The immortal mind that hath forsook
> Her mansion in this fleshly nook:
> And of those *Daemons* that are found
> In fire, air, flood, or under ground,
> Whose power hath a true consent
> With Planet, or with Element.
>
> [87-96]

The russet lawns and fallows gray of L'Allegro's field of vision have yielded their underlying essences to Il Penseroso.
As he outwatches, unspheres, and unfolds the great cosmic
display above him, as he penetrates the "true consent" of the
four elements that constitute his earthly home, the pensive
man climbs to the heights of the lofty knowledge that
characterizes our notion of the divinely inspired Miltonic
poet.

By paralleling Il Penseroso's active contemplation, so to
call it, of the divine universal plan with L'Allegro's corresponding pastoral promenade, Milton invites comparison.
Judgments between the two experiences are irresistible when
the poems present such incompatible standards, and so it is
not easily possible to hold the two poems in equilibrium like
unrelated *Weltanschauungen*. If we decide that Milton's
lifelong concern with the moral impact of choice
predominates over any balance that the two experiences may
suggest, the earlier life-style of *L'Allegro* yields before the

sober, mysterious vision of *Il Penseroso*.

A parallel to this moral shift from one poem to the next is suggested by Virgil in the second *Georgic*, the panegyric on country life. As Maren-Sophie Røstvig has demonstrated, this poem is part of a continuing tradition in itself, often apart from the pastoral, in praise of the joys of rural labor and retirement.[38] At one point Virgil's *beatus vir* breaks away from his praise of the georgic life and utters this hope:

> My fondest prayer is that the Muses dear,
> Life's joy supreme, may take me to their choir,
> Their priest, by boundless ecstasy possessed.
> The heavenly secrets may they show, the stars,
> Eclipses of the sun, the ministries
> Of the laborious moon, why quakes the earth,
> And by what power, the oceans fathomless
> Rise, bursting every bound, then sink away
> To their own bed. . . .
>
> [475-83]

The secrets of the heavens, revealed by the patronage of the Muses, far surpass for Virgil's speaker, as for Il Penseroso, the joys of the landscape. In fact, Virgil's speaker is willing to settle for less. If he cannot be admitted to the mysterious domain of the heavens, then, like L'Allegro, he will go back to the landscape;

> . . . if the blood
> Flows not so potent in my colder breast,
> Make me true lover of fair field and farm,
> Of streams in dewy vales. . . .

Milton establishes a hierarchical structure in the value scale of the twin poems similar to Virgil's, as the perspective shifts upwards from the pleasures of Mirth to those of Melancholy. As he himself had said in the Seventh Prolusion:

> Again, if the happiness of the life that we live among men

consists in the mind's honest and liberal pleasure, then the delights that are the secret of study and learning as such easily surpass all others. How much it means to grasp all the principles of the heavens and their stars, all the movements and disturbances of the atmosphere.[39]

Looking from earth to heaven, man exercises his potentiality to raise himself through the cosmic hierarchy.

In the fourth section (96-120) Il Penseroso matches L'Allegro's earlier description of the country stories and romantic tales of chivalry. The pensive version, of course, is of a more somber hue: he invites "Gorgeous Tragedy" (97) to sweep before him and recalls the "sage and solemn tunes" (117) of great bards. He concerns himself once again with the profounder significance in his experience: the tourneys and trophies in his world must present "more . . . than meets the ear" (120). In this section of the poem Il Penseroso summons up the Orpheus image, significantly altering that flexible fable from the use to which L'Allegro put it. It no longer concludes the poem, and its emphasis falls on Orpheus's power as a successful singer.[40] Unlike the earlier Orpheus, who failed to raise Eurydice from the dead, this Orpheus is remembered as the poet who

> Drew Iron tears down *Pluto*'s cheeck,
> And made Hell grant what Love did seek.
>
> [107-08]

It is worth recalling that Orpheus has also reversed his original passive role in *L'Allegro*, where he merely heard the strains of hidden harmony, and now strongly sings his redemptive song before Pluto.[41]

With the dawn comes the final section of the poem (121-74), considerably longer than the corresponding section in its companion. In *L'Allegro* the final lines were concerned with the effect of "soft *Lydian* airs" (136) on the poetic sensibility. In keeping with the emphasis that Il Penseroso has placed on the deeper meaning of the surface experience of L'Allegro's world, the pensive man echoes the themes of the earlier poem while imbuing them with his own special insight. The most obvious instance of this process is found in Il Penseroso's invocation to music. Where L'Allegro desired to be lapped in the sensual sweetness of music, the pensive man aspires to witness the

> . . . pealing Organ blow,
> To the full voic'd Quire below,
> In Service High, and Anthems cleer.
>
> [161-63]

The pagan inspiration of the earlier poem is abandoned in favor of the Christian religious music that will bring the beatific vision before the pensive man's eyes. It is significant, incidentally, that Milton repeats in *Il Penseroso*'s visionary conclusion a pattern of light and sound imagery similar to that in the ode. All heaven will be brought before Il Penseroso's "eyes" through the agency of religious music apprehended through his "ear." Music once again acts as the agent of religious ecstasy.

The lower order of pastoral nature also forms a part of the conclusion. For twenty-five lines of this section (121-45) Il Penseroso moves through the "twilight groves" (133) of the overhanging forest. As he enters the "Hollow'd haunt" (138) that nature provides as a shelter, he hears the "rocking Winds . . . Piping loud" (126) that anticipate the pealing organ of his final ecstasy. The music of nature harmonizes with his contemplative disposition:

> . . . the Bee with Honied thie
> That at her flowry work doth sing,
> And the Waters murmuring
> With such consort as they keep,
> Entice the dewy-feather'd Sleep.
>
> [142-46]

Milton's inspiration in this section was perhaps derived from a similar description of the rural pleasures that attend Tityrus in Virgil's first *Eclogue* (51-58), the importance of which I noted in Chapter 1. The seclusion which marks the situation of both Tityrus and Il Penseroso is softened and enhanced by the protective harmony of the elements acting in concert to lull the retired man to rest. When experienced by the contemplative mind, pastoral carries with it the Virgilian associations of moral quietude and genuine *otium*.

The picture that the pensive man paints of the forest recalls the central pastoral section of *L'Allegro*. In *Il Penseroso*, though, there is a difference. Nature is "hallow'd" so that no "profaner eye" (140) can look upon her unsullied charms. The suggestion that the forest anticipates the "high embowed Roof" (157) of the ecstatic vision and that the sounds of nature harmonize with the sound of choral voices injects a sacred element into nature, an admittedly unusual one for the early Milton, but rhetorically effective nonetheless. The earlier pastoral descriptions of *L'Allegro* conveyed an impression of mere surface beauty. If nature was a manifestation of the spirit, the cheerful man did not apprehend it. The landscape for *Il Penseroso*, on the other hand, holds within it the path to divine contemplation. Its hallowed sounds, "sent by som spirit to mortals good" (153) leads him "to walk the studious Cloysters pale" (156). Once again we find him moving actively in search of his vision. The difference between Milton's two versions of pastoral in *L'Allegro-Il Penseroso* underlines his conception of the differences between the two views of life that the poems present. This difference is accentuated by the position of the pastoral section in the structure of each poem. In *L'Allegro* the pastoral description is centrally placed and symbolic of its speaker's sensibility. In *Il Penseroso* the pastoral description is peripheral to the speaker's fullest revelations of his own particular sensibility. His echo of L'Allegro's pastoral description is penultimate to his concluding hope that he shall one day dissolve into ecstasies and attain the prophetic voice. His stay in the covert groves of the forest only anticipates the "Hairy Gown and Mossy Cell" (169) of a more prolonged and satisfying contemplative life. The futurity of the poem's concluding lines, where Il Penseroso anticipates his imaginative growth into vatic power, is as characteristic of Milton as the muted vision they depict. The "peacefull hermitage" (168) of his old age provides none of the "wanton heed, and giddy cunning" that L'Allegro so fervently desires. Whereas we left the cheerful man facing an aimless future, the pensive man foresees a life of active contemplation, studying

> . . . every Star that Heav'n doth shew,
> And every Herb that sips the dew.
>
> [171-72]

Like the narrator of the ode, he places himself between the stars of heaven and the herbs of the earth, mediating both in the realm of his imagination.

# 4

## Spenser, Milton, and the Pastoral Elegy

$T$*he* pastoral elegies of Spenser and Milton offer a rare opportunity to assay their mutual ambitions and differing imaginative orientations from an unusually concentrated and
critically wieldy perspective. *Lycidas* and "November,"
both imperishable fruits of this curious branch of the pastoral
tree, inevitably have invited comparison, usually as a means
of accounting for the complexities of Milton's greatest short
poem.[1] Both of these elegies, as well as *Astrophel* and
*Epitaphium Damonis*, belong to one another as members of a
pastoral family. Such a trope is not unwarranted: the pastoral
elegy, of course, descends in a direct lineage from
Theocritus's first *Idyl*, and each new addition to the mode is
engendered with dutiful attention to its distinguished
forebears. Few other verse forms demand of the poet such
rigorous observance of prescribed, inherited conventions.[2]
Indeed, the pastoral elegy challenges the poet not merely to
overgo his predecessors, but virtually to animate the stylizations and artifice of an exceptionally limited mode of utterance. The exacting poetic codes of the pastoral elegy, its
conventions, constitute an end in themselves. We cannot skim

116

off the conventions to find the "emotion" of the poem beneath a thick overlay of self-conscious literary plaster. Such reductive critical techniques, never commendable, are especially unconscionable with regard to the pastoral elegy, where the poet has clearly set out to discipline his talents according to the prescribed formulae arrayed before him in narrow literary channels. For these reasons, then, we may now approach Spenser and Milton in a manageably comparative fashion that allows sharper attention to each poet's intricate manipulation of his imaginative material. The questions that their pastoral elegies raise take us beyond those which the previous two chapters have pondered about the poet's vocational vicissitudes. The pastoral elegies consistently demand that we ask how the poet evokes a response from his reader and what kind of a response it is. How does the elegist wrench from a time-worn, stylized set of conventions a satisfying utterance about death's merciless instrusion upon youth in full bloom? What may we learn about the poet's imaginative processes from his scrupulous adaptation of the pastoral machinery to express sudden horror before the spectre of brutal, senseless death?

In feeling our way toward the elusive relationship between "convention" and "emotion," it may be helpful to recall that it is a singularly modern disposition which questions the relationship as a problematic one. In his "Notes on Convention," Harry Levin wisely reminds us that "we are still the heirs of the romanticists, and our basic unit of aesthetic discussion is still personality."[3] If we fail to distinguish the poet's personal expression, as we moderns know it, from the reader's emotional response stimulated by convention, we cannot justly appreciate the pastoral elegy. The successful pastoral elegist shifts the burden of personal emotion away from his "personality" and embodies the emotion within the artifact of his poem. The observation is not intended to deny the individual identities of Spenser's and Milton's pastoral elegists, who present themselves before us with distinctive voices, tones, and attitudes. It is rather to assert that the elegist employs his pastoral conventions in a fashion that forces us radically to disembody the poem from the sensibilities of both poet and reader, persuading us to contemplate it as an artifact of deeply ambiguous significance to our extra-aesthetic lives. This disembodiment is endemic to the *pastoral* elegy in ways that sharply distinguish the mode from even the nonpastoral elegy. For example, consider Bishop King's *The Exequy*. Like any of its pastoral counterparts, this beautiful poem is imbued with conventions; it is constructed entirely on a host of witty conceits fashionable in midcentury. And it progresses as staunchly as *Lycidas* does to a concluding Christian consolation. Yet I dare say that King's elegy stirs in us emotions far tenderer than Milton's poem does, and forges a deeply sympathetic bond between the elegist and the reader. Nobody, so far as I know, has written a pastoral elegy to bemoan the death of his spouse or child. This is because, at its best, the pastoral elegy does not, cannot, should not deploy its conventions chiefly to express hard, intimately subjective grief.

The pastoral elegy is a form of literary ritual, whose speaker presents himself in a priestlike posture, and whose conventions serve the same function that the liturgy serves in the religious ritual. Recognizing the liturgical character of the elegy's conventions, the reader responds to their artifice much as a participant in the religious ritual responds to the artifice of the liturgy; that is, he accepts them as necessary to the enactment of a ritual that is beyond our capacity to account for within the limits of our daily experience. Analogous to the continual reenactment of the liturgy, the continual reanimation of the conventions of the pastoral elegy responds to the human need to fathom the mystery of life and death within the larger patterns of the race and the eternal laws of nature. The pastoral elegy confronts death at the heart of the natural cycle and ritualizes death and the emotions it arouses.

At this point we may turn to Northrop Frye, whose

deliberations on convention in *The Anatomy of Criticism*, however we may respond to his critical philosophy as a methodology, state the matter with the utmost pertinence to the pastoral elegy. Starting from the conviction that a study of genres has to be founded on a study of the recurring conventions which integrate and unify literary experience, Frye asserts that recurrent acts of symbolic communication enact rituals and that critical analysis deals with literature "in terms of the generic, recurring, or conventional actions which show analogies to rituals: the weddings, funerals, intellectual and social initiations, . . . and so on." He proceeds:

> The principle of recurrence in the rhythm of art seems to be derived from the repetitions in nature that make time intelligible to us. Rituals cluster around the cyclical movements of the sun, the moon, the seasons, and human life. Every crucial periodicity of experience: dawn, sunset, the phases of the moon, seed-time and harvest, the equinoxes and solstices, birth, initiation, marriage, and death, get rituals attached to them.[4]

The most accomplished examples of the pastoral elegy confront death by defining its meaning according to the cyclical movements of the landscape. The conventions of the elegy allow—indeed, demand—that the poet enlarge the painful experience of grief under the aspect of cyclical decline and renewal. Within the ritualized confinements of the elegy, the poet forms a social bond with his reader, analogous to the bond between priest and worshiper; the pastoral elegy (as Frye observes of drama) "like the ritual in religion is primarily a social or ensemble performance."[5] Having contrived that bond, the elegist is able to persuade his audience of the efficacy of his art. His unique power to enlarge the scope of human experience allows him to evoke—as all rituals do—the mythic past for the purpose of reconstructing and reordering the future. But the evocation of the mythic past can only find in idyllic human genesis an ironic and poignant reminder of the change that death has wrought. "The bucolic mind," as Renato Poggioli has said, "realizes that nature is not only a provider but also a destroyer, generating from its womb forces hindering life as well as fostering it."[6] Correspondingly, then, seasonal rotation and the cyclical renewal of nature encourage a hope for human renewal, rebirth, redemption.

The pagan elegist, however, does not articulate his awareness of past felicity as fully as the modern elegist, an awareness most perfectly realized when the speaker of *Lycidas* summons up his idyllic boyhood of fresh dews and battening flocks. Neither Theocritus nor Virgil elaborates on the harmony that sustained life before Daphnis's death (although each poet strongly suggests a lost prelapsarian bliss when his elegist cries out for nature to reverse her wonted peaceful curse and to pervert her processes in response to Daphnis's death). Accordingly, the modern pastoral elegy also deviates from its classical counterpart in its powerful affirmative conclusion. Both the idyllic past and the promise of spiritual rebirth, the mythic loci of the Christian ethos, are only partly delineated in, say, Virgil's celebration of Daphnis. By virtue of his religious beliefs, the Christian elegist is thrust into a more complex situation than his classical precursors, whereby he is more sensitive to the nuances and ironies of temporality. He mediates between the past, when a slumber sealed his spirit from the grief of loss and death, and a yet more joyous future. As a midway terrain of the present, suspended moment, his poem depicts a temporal vista along which the elegist recollects the innocent past and, with another ritualistic movement, envisions a horizon of timeless bliss. The elegy, then, not only enacts the power of the poet's imagination to depict the dead shepherd in eternal glory; it also demonstrates his sacramental power to heal the spirit of grief-ravaged man. In the pagan elegy, on the other hand, the poet's vision affects man less than it does nature: at the end of Virgil's fifth *Eclogue*, for example, the landscape is calmed and reorchestrated under the new harmony initiated by Daphnis's ascent. In both pagan and modern elegies, though, the balancing temporal fields of pastoral serenity that surround the performance of the elegy highlight the present moment of ritual, when past and future merge in the verbal act, conferring upon the elegy its efficacy.

For all of these important affinities, the tradition from its beginnings has always accommodated two quite different strains. The first strain, which I have dwelt upon so far, I shall call the orphic elegy. Its heroes include Moschus's Bion, Virgil's Daphnis, and Milton's Lycidas. All three are celebrated for their poetic powers, and each is announced as the successor of Orpheus himself. The elegist stresses the poetic bonds that unite him with the dead shepherd hero; often this bond is that of mentor to disciple. Even in the pagan orphic elegy, the poet himself assures us of the resurrection of the dead shepherd, an assurance that invariably guarantees the elegy to be a triumphant hymn of joy. What we think of as personal, subjective grief is subsumed by a literary ritual whose character is most clearly manifested in the sharply liturgical movement from woe to joy. Besides this ritualism, a further mark of the religious quality of the strain is exhibited in the enchanting effect of the dead shepherd's influence on the processes of the landscape. Most of all, the orphic elegy displays perennial concern with the art of poetry and the role of the poet. As the hymn is sung, the dead shepherd's garland of laurel passes to the brows of his elegist, so that the movement from death to life is maintained within the very confines of the poem. D. C. Allen's remark on *Lycidas* applies aptly to all orphic elegies: "It is a sort of analogy that Milton found unavoidable: Christ-Orpheus-Milton."[7] The performance of the elegy itself offers irresistible proof that the orphic shepherd-poet lives on in the person of his elegist. Moreover, the final apotheosis succeeds and convinces us precisely because of the elegist's priestlike posture. His ultimate apotheotic vision, if he has persuaded us of his sacramental powers, is unimpeachable and satisfying.

The second and perhaps less clearly defined strain I shall call the adonean elegy. It is represented most clearly in the personages of Bion's Adonis, Virgil's Gallus, Spenser's Astrophel, and Milton's Damon. The lamented shepherd-hero is not remembered primarily as a poet, serving as an inspiration to, or predecessor of, the elegist, but as a personal friend for whose loss there can be granted little consolation. The dead shepherd may have been a poet, of course, but his relationship to the elegist is portrayed first and foremost as an intimate one of man to friend. Far from presenting itself as a ritualistic celebration of the godlike powers of the poet-hero, the adonean elegy enacts the personal, painful lament of one man for the loss of another. This intensely subjective note proves to be the nemesis of the adonean elegy, because this strain often adheres with equal (and, as we shall see, irreconcilable) zeal to the pastoral elegiac convention that dictates a joyous apotheosis. Principally for this reason, the adonean strain, when measured against the orphic, is ultimately unsuccessful. The final consolation in the adonean elegy, if it exists at all, either fails to convince or is patently inappropriate to the poem as a whole. In the pagan examples under consideration, Bion's *Lament for Adonis* and Virgil's tribute to Gallus, the *consolatio* is so slight as to be negligible. The adonean elegies of Spenser and Milton follow their pagan precursors, but usually append an inappropriate (albeit orthodoxly unexceptionable) Christian *consolatio*. Although the motif of poetry and the poet's special powers may be fond in the adonean elegy, this theme is neither central nor coherently worked out, because the elegist overridingly proclaims his grief, not his efficacious art. In the end, the adonean elegy leaves an impression of starkly disconsolate loss that the poem has proved powerless to relieve, whatever its stated intention. The future looms ahead bleakly bereft of the lost shepherd for whose death there can be found no real reparation.

The orphic elegy arises, as previous discussion has shown, from the enchantments that its prototypical singer was said to exercise over the landscape. As the poet-priest par excellence, whose powers were thought to have suppressed natural disorder and encouraged the flourishing of civilization, Orpheus persisted even into the Renaissance to attract poets convinced of their own spiritual brotherhood with him.[8] In the pastoral elegy, of course, of primary interest is Orpheus's violent death at the frenzied hands of the Maenads. The tragedy of his story is overshadowed, however, by his achievement in bringing art to nature, and the perpetuation of his memory is ensured by the continual reenactment of his sacramental and civilizing poetry. He is remembered, then, whether as a *theologos*, who sang of the origins of the world, or as the archetypal pastoral poet, chiefly for his mysterious vatic powers. Those pastoral elegies over which he presides are sung, we could say, in his honor, as testimony to the power of the poet to give shape to human experience, to find the source of civilization in the midst of nature, to impart his wisdom to his fellowman.

The myth of Adonis is of quite another stamp. At first a cult hero whose destruction and renewal corresponded to seasonal change, Adonis was gradually transformed into the youthful adventurer whose violent death at the tusk of the boar incited grievous lamentation. Even today, thanks to Shakespeare's poem, he is remembered primarily for his beauty and for the grief his death brought to Aphrodite. Every springtime, according to his chroniclers, he is mourned anew on the feast of the Adonia.[9] The importance of Adonis in the pastoral elegy does not derive from his attraction as the inspirational prototype for future poets. He is not celebrated so much as lamented. Just as the Orpheus legend figures selectively in the pastoral elegy to stress the hero's poetic gifts over his failure as the lover of Eurydice, so too the pastoral elegy consistently disregards Adonis's seasonal renewal in favor of the more lugubrious aspects of his legend. He is remembered intimately and sadly as the lost lover, the youthful adventurer cut down in his prime. In Virgil's Gallus *Eclogue* (1.18) and in Theocritus's first *Idyl* (1.109), Adonis makes his only appearance in either poet's pastoral canon, and in each case he is designated a shepherd. His legend survives in the Renaissance to haunt Ronsard's *Adonis*, Spenser's *Astrophel*, and even *Epitaphium Damonis*, never as the orphic precursor of poetry, but as the prototypical shepherd victim whose death is violently bemoaned and for whose loss there is no real solace.

It will be useful to consider briefly several of the important classical funeral elegies from which Spenser and Milton derive their contributions to the mode. Two poems commonly yoked, Bion's *Lament for Adonis* and Moschus's *Lament for Bion*, present with admirable clarity the differences between the orphic and adonean strains that later and greater poets enrich.[10] Bion's poem, probably composed for the Adonia,[11] extravagantly bewails the loss of the mythological huntsman and makes no attempt to assuage the grief that his violent death has incited. Although Poggioli posits that the poem transcends the pastoral canon because "the pity the poet conveys is directed more to the bereaved mistress than to the dead youth,"[12] it cannot be denied that the *Lament* flourishes several pastoral conventions that recur in centuries to come: the refrain ("I weep for Adonis, fair Adonis is dead"); the pathetic fallacy and the disruption of nature; the trooping of the divinities to the grave of the dead huntsman. Prefiguring *Astrophel*, the elegist recounts the gruesome details of the death and Cypris's subsequent, flamboyant grief. Rivers weep, the woods cry out, and flowers grow red in sorrow: these are standard features of the pastoral elegy. Bion's distinct contribution lies in the purpose of the elegy: it is written to foment sorrow; we are asked to experience the horror of bereavement without the solace of ritualized consolation. The poet offers us, therefore, no apotheosis, no comfort, no balm whatever. In fact, he deliberately aggravates distress by concluding the poem with what appears, by hindsight, to be an ironic parody of the traditional *consolatio* that envisions a hopeful future:

> Enough tears, Cytherea, enough for today.
> No more wailing now or beating your breast.
> There is time enough to come for your grief,
> time to weep, time to sorrow, as year succeeds year.[13]

As we shall see, Bion's bleak *Lament* finds its descendents not only in the curious *Alcon* of Castiglione, but also in Spenser's and Milton's elegies.

Bion's poem differs from Moschus's *Lament for Bion* in that the later poem, probably written by a disciple of Bion, takes as its subject an actual man known to the elegist himself. Paradoxically, though, the dead Bion is portrayed not in the form of an actual human being, like the mythological Adonis in the earlier poem. The hero of Moschus's elegy is mourned as a poet whose primordial rhythms seemed to animate the landscape. No display of personal grief, like that of Cypris's mourning for Adonis, enlivens this elegy. Instead, the poet substitutes a highly exaggerated fanfare of the pathetic fallacy, presumably in order to emphasize the extensive effects of the poet's death. Because this elegy is the first in which the dead shepherd is directly endowed with poetic laurels and the first in which the elegist appropriates the poetic mantle for his own shoulders,[14] references to Orpheus abound almost naturally. The most significant reference occurs at the beginning of the poem, when the elegist pointedly claims that "the Doric Orpheus is dead." Even the refrain, which in Bion's earlier lament simply stated, "I weep for Adonis; fair Adonis is dead," is calculated to draw attention away from personal grief and toward the poetic role of the dead shepherd (and of the elegist): "Sing, Sicilian muses, raise your song of grief," cries

the elegist. This theme runs consistently through to the end of
the poem with its muted statement of consolation. Bion is not
dead, we are told, because the sound of his music will live on.
The elegist is

> . . . no stranger
> to pastoral song, but a pupil of yours,
> an heir to your Dorian style,
> honoured, when others inherited
> your wealth, to be left your music.

Poggioli claims that a crown of laurel for the elegist cannot
compensate for Bion's death and that Bion's reintegration into the natural processes constitutes a weak promise of immortality.[15] Although his observations would be valid if the poem
had been composed chiefly to lament a dead friend, they fall
slightly off center when we consider that the elegist exhibits as
much concern for his own song as he does for the loss of
Bion. For this elegist, Bion, whether dead or alive, appears to
have no identity apart from his poetic art, an identity,
moreover, which lives on even as the elegy unfolds. The closing lines of the poem confirm that the energies of the elegist
are divided at least equally between vaunting his own artistry
and celebrating the lost poet:

> As once she granted Orpheus, for the rhythms
> of his harp, the return of his Eurydice,
> So shall [Persephone] return you, Bion, to the hills.
> Could my pipe ever match the magic of his harp
> I would myself have sung for you to Hades.

Having completely abandoned his pretense of grief, the
elegist verifies what has been suspiciously close to the surface
throughout the poem, that his own art and pastoral career
serve as his main preoccupation. It is difficult otherwise to
account for the overwrought exhibition of the pathetic fallacy
pervading the poem. By stretching this frail convention
almost to the point of absurdity, the elegist primarily calls

our attention to his purple skills.

If Milton, or Spenser, or any other Renaissance poet had had only Moschus and Bion as his precursors, the pastoral elegy would have remained confined to antiquity. I have discussed their seminal contributions to the mode, not merely to indicate their limitations, but to suggest how a great poet can transmute even a debased tradition. For there can be no doubt that by the time Virgil wrote the fifth *Eclogue*, in imitation of Theocritus, the pastoral elegy already constituted a tradition, maintained by Moschus and Bion. In his fifth and tenth *Eclogues* Virgil provides distinguished examples of the orphic and adonean elegies respectively, molding into imitable shape the material bequeathed him by tradition.

The fifth *Eclogue*, presided over by that mysterious successor of Orpheus, the primordial Daphnis, exemplifies literary ritual in its most accomplished form.[16] Virgil's initial device to ensure the success of this ritual places the dual performance of the elegiac songs within the framework of a friendly conversation between two shepherds. We are led into the funeral rite genially, then, by following the cheerful debate between Mopsus and Menalcas on the kinds of song they might sing. By refusing to overwhelm the reader with a direct lament and by detaching the performance of the elegy from the emotional compulsions that usually attend death, the poet elicits from his reader a trusting disposition that will willingly follow wherever the poet wishes to lead. Each singer intones twenty-four lines, comprising counterbalancing sections of lament and joy. First Mopsus mourns the demise of Daphnis, outlines his extraordinary gifts, and describes the universal grief of nature at his death. Like Orpheus, Daphnis had the ability to yoke the Armenian tigers and tame the Bacchic revellers. His importance for the well-being of the landscape is reflected not only in the catastrophic effect that his death induced, when the crops died and the cattle abstained from water, but also in the similes that the elegist chooses to honor the dead hero. As vines adorn the trees, so Daphnis adorns all around him (*vitis ut arboris decori est . . . tu decus omne tuis*) 32-34. Mopsus culminates his lament with an epitaph that announces Daphnis's universal fame. Daphnis, he says, commanded these funeral rites in his own memory (*mandat fieri sibi talia Daphnis*) 41. Having heard Mopsus's conclusion, Menalcas rejoices in his comrade's performance and proclaims him *divina poeta*, bestowing the mantle of the dead shepherd himself upon his fellow elegist. We learn that Daphnis led them in song and that they now style themselves his disciples (49-52).

Menalcas's rite follows immediately, abruptly switching Mopsus's dirge into a hieratic hymn of joy. As he begins, Menalcas leaves no doubt that his song will be responsible for Daphnis's apotheosis:

> nos tamen haec quocumque modo tibi nostra vicissim
> dicemus, Daphnimque tuum tollemus ad astra;
> Daphnim ad astra feremus . . . .

> Still, here's a song of my own I'll give you in return, as best I may, raising your Daphnis to the stars. Yes, I will set him there among the stars. . . .
>
> [50-52]

As Daphnis is translated to the outer reaches of the galaxy, the elegist's imagination expands to encompass the entire cosmos. The hero's apotheosis has the expected beneficent effect on nature, and the universal lament depicted earlier by Mopsus is now transformed into universal harmony. Images of the golden age are invoked to illustrate how the landscape rejoices in Daphnis's elevation, for Daphnis loves idyllic peace (*amat bonus otia Daphnis*) 61. Pastoral harmony, we are led to conclude, far from being shattered by Daphnis's death, has been strengthened and renewed by his resurrection. He becomes a god ("*deus, deus ille, Menalca*," nature cries) 64, to whom the singers promise perpetual prayer and sacrificial devotion. His spirit survives in the *otium* of the landscape as well as in the communal priesthood that his death has ordained for his two disciples, a bond demonstrated in their exchange of gifts.

At the same time that the elegy exhibits all the traits of the ritualistic celebration of the orphic singer, it strengthens the claims of the powers of the poetic imagination.[17] We are encouraged to accept the sharp movement from dirge to hymn, paralleled by Daphnis's own movement from earth to the heavens, because we are never allowed to forget that we are participating in a deliberate, finely crafted, imaginative ritual. The elegy bears the orphic hallmark of conventions so detached from common reality that we surrender any literal-minded doubts we may ordinarily harbor about the poet's claims for his art. At the end of the poem we are able to accept as an imaginative assertion that the mediating power of the two priestly elegists has affirmed Daphnis's stature as a poetic divinity.

These observations can be measured if we pause for a moment over Virgil's adonean elegy, the tenth *Eclogue*. The poem is not strictly an elegy: like Theocritus's Daphnis, its hero, the soldier-poet Gallus, does not actually die in the poem, but rather looks forward to death from love's agonies. Even if we cannot categorize it unequivocally as an elegy, it has nonetheless been taken as such by Virgil's successors, notably in *Lycidas*. And there is good reason to read the *Eclogue* as a lament, for Gallus's sorrow suggests death more than love or life. The real test of the poem's predominant mood comes after Gallus has voiced his woe, when the Arcadian poet himself, promising that his love for his friend will continue to grow (*amor tantum mihi crescit in horas*) 73, concludes with these melancholy lines:

> surgamus: solet esse gravis cantantibus umbra,
> iuniperi gravis umbra, nocent et frugibus umbrae.
> ite domum saturae, venit Hesperus, ite capellae.

Now let us go. The shade is bad for singers. This is a
juniper: its shade is bad. Even crops suffer in the shade.
Home with you, goats: you have had your fill. Hesper is
coming: home with you goats.

[75-77]

These final lines may or may not be Virgil's conscious
leave-taking of pastoral.[18] In either case, they convey the
frustration and loss of the adonean elegy. Gallus's anxieties
for the mistress who has deserted him have propelled his fan-
tasies into the freezing mountains and arid deserts where he
threatens to die. Because the sleet and snow of Macedonia
and the tropical sun of Ethiopia belong in our own uncomfortable world, Gallus's phantasms increase the distance between the idyllic pleasance of the *Eclogues* and the mortal woe
of history. As Bruno Snell has pointed out, Gallus is the only
actually historical figure in the *Eclogues*, and therefore he
represents all of us cut off from Arcadia. [19] His solitude and
his bleak concluding vision override any claims the Arcadian
poet asserts for continuing concern on Gallus's behalf.
Besides, the Arcadian poet admits that his poetic *fiscella*, his
mallow basket, intricate and frail, has diverted him from his
friend's sorrow. Gallus's lonely posture reflects the familiar
adonean one of the mourner, forever separate from the
desired object. Bereavement, loss, and disunity are the
keynotes; Gallus's future is empty of the spiritual bonds of
peace that characterize Virgil's earlier elegy.

Virgil's followers in the Renaissance drew on the Gallus
*Eclogue* repeatedly, whenever, for instance, they deployed
the convention of the divinities marching to the grave of the
dead shepherd. *Lycidas*, to choose an obvious example,
models itself on the tenth *Eclogue* in its pattern of invocation, lament, and eight-line conclusion.[20] But Virgil's
Daphnis *Eclogue* penetrated the Renaissance poet's sensibility
much more sharply than the Gallus. The reason for this is obvious: the Christian poet was far more prepared to imitate the

Daphnis elegy with its concluding joyous apotheosis than the melancholy ending of the tenth *Eclogue*. For the Middle Ages the messianic *Eclogue* had helped to sanctify its author as an unwitting herald of Christianity; the fifth as readily adapted itself to the Renaissance elegist's belief in the transcendence of death through Christian faith. The precedent that Menalcas established when he enthroned Daphnis among the stars encouraged the Renaissance elegist eager to put his talents to the test in a public display that announces his responsibility as the tamer of woe and harmonizer of chaos.

Spenser's finest orphic elegy, "November," enacts vividly the patterns of the ritualistic lament. Earlier we had occasion to deliberate on the elegy for Dido in the context of Colin's story in the *Calender*. It is not inappropriate now, then, to sunder the poem from its local habitation and to place it in the tradition from which it derives. One remarkable aspect of "November," however, is that, for all its affinities with Virgil's fifth *Eclogue*, Spenser at this point in his career had hardly been touched by Virgil's direct influence. As Merritt Hughes years ago demonstrated, it is impossible to locate a single passage in the *Calender* indebted to Virgil's example.[21] That Spenser modeled his elegy on Marot's *De Madame Loyse* demonstrates, we may say, an object lesson in the power of the tradition, whereby even its remotest or most indirect descendents share with its founders similar attitudes and traits. Spenser shares with Virgil the detached tone, the ritualized formulae, the remarkably impersonal mood paradoxically capable of transmitting such emotional energy. A conversational framework also encloses the performance of Spenser's elegy, encouraging us, as in Virgil, to participate in the ritual from a distance, to detach our emotional response to it from our daily lives and intercourse.

On the other hand, Spenser's elegy securely represents its author, and we may best construe its place in the tradition by noting at once in which ways "November" differs from

Virgil's elegy. Why, for instance, does Colin sing this lament? We know that Mopsus and Menalcas sang Daphnis's elegy because the dead shepherd hero had commanded them to do so in his memory; the two swains inherited Daphnis's orphic powers. If Thenot, say, who encourages Colin to bewail Dido's death, had instead himself sung an elegy for the dead *Colin*, then the similarities between Virgil and Spenser would have been conveniently clear. As it is, Colin's reason for singing his lament, as it is explained in the framework of the poem, is much more contrived and even less "personal" than that of Mopsus and Menalcas. Thenot maintains that Colin ought to recover his lost talents by creating a song "whose endles souenaunce/Emong the shepeheards swaines may aye remaine"(5-6). There is barely a suggestion in the expressed motivation for the song that Colin himself will achieve renown, much less immortality, by means of his song. It is the poem itself, endlessly reenacted, that will "aye remaine." In this way throughout the long framework, as Colin and Thenot debate the propriety of singer and subject, Spenser takes pains to ensure that we resist interpreting this elegy as an expression of Colin's personal feelings. Furthermore, Thenot has encouraged Colin to begin his song with the offer of a remuneration, "yond Cosset"(42), which is dutifully presented at the close of the eclogue. In Virgil the gift-giving was an exchange between friends, an outward and visible sign of their brotherhood in Daphnis. In Spenser the gift-giving is a reward for services rendered. A poet in shepherd's guise is commissioned to apply his well-known skills to a subject dear to his listener's heart; the poet-shepherd's labors must be recompensed materially. This theme has just been clearly stated in "October"; it is given particular expression in pastoral terms now in "November." But the poet's labors must also be worth the reward: we had "better learne of hem, that learned bee," says Thenot, "and han be watered at the Muses well" (29-30). He speaks justly, for instruction—*utile*—motivates Colin's song. At the end of his elegy, he has imparted his wisdom and speaks on behalf of all his listeners, when he asserts

> Now haue I learnd (a lesson derely bought)
> That nys on earth assuraunce to be sought.
>
> [156-57]

The framework further defines Colin's elegy as a literary ritual by reminding us that the dreary time of the year requires an appropriately melancholy song: "Thilke sollein season sadder plight doth aske" (17). In the same way, Dido herself, as she is presented in the elegy, personifies the dying season. In furnishing Colin with necessary biographical information about her, Thenot claims that Dido was the daughter of the "greate shepehearde" (38), a plain allusion (despite E. Ko's admonition to the contrary) to Pan himself. Dido's role, therefore, is emblematic of the intimacy between man and nature. Her place in this elegy cannot be fully valued apart from her ritualized attachment to the seasonal rotation of the landscape. To grant Dido this universal significance allows us to regard both the elegy and the meaning of her death from a widely philosophical vantage point. By closely associating Dido with the very forces of nature—

> The earth now lacks her wonted light,
> And all we dwell in deadly night—
>
> [68-69]

Spenser successfully transforms the precarious device of the pathetic fallacy into a suitable ritual lament for the loss of nature's sustaining power, personified by Dido.[22]

The elegy itself begins after Colin assumes the role of the ritual leader of public mourning, summoning the "mournefulst Muse of nyne" (53). After the self-reflective invocation, "Vp grieslie ghostes and vp my rufull ryme" (55), he then turns to his (presumably) imagined audience and addresses them in these commandingly liturgical cadences:

> Shepheards, that by your flocks on Kentish downes
>     abyde,
> Waile ye this wofull waste of natures warke:
> Waile we the wight, whose presence was our pryde:
> Waile we the wight, whose absence is out carke.
> The sonne of all the world is dimme and darke.
>
> [63-67]

By first using the imperative "Waile ye . . ." and by then expanding to the first person plural, "Waile we . . .," Colin consolidates his authority as the representative celebrant of this litany-like performance. He thus permits himself to ask and answer rhetorical questions on broad metaphysical topics:

> Why wayle we then? Why weary we the Gods with
>     playnts,
> As if some euill were to her betight?
> She raignes a goddesse now emong the saintes,
> That whilome was the saynt of shepheards light.
>
> [173-76]

These questions would have been out of place in Virgil's elegy for Daphnis, because of the earlier poem's more rigid movement from sorrow to joy in the separate songs of its two speakers. Spenser not only provides a single elegist who must incorporate both emotions successively, but also takes trouble to stress his elegist's relationship to his audience. Mopsus and Menalcas have only each other as immediate listeners. Colin's tone forces us to postulate, in addition to Thenot, a much wider public reception for his performance. Spenser's elegist sings representatively to, as well as for, a general, unseen audience. We picture him in an arena far larger than that of the pastoral environment:

> Vnwise and wretched men to weete whats good or ill,
> We deeme of Death as doome of ill desert:

But knewe we fooles, what it vs bringes vntil,
Dye would we dayly, once it to expert.

[183-86]

The medieval homilitic tradition, his words remind us, has intervened between Virgil and Spenser and has placed the elegist in a pulpit before a congregation. Virgil's priestly elegists with their private, sacramental devotion to Daphnis have been transformed by Spenser, we may say, into the more Protestant and preacherly elegist of "November."

Discussing "November" earlier as part of the *Calender*, I observed that one of the poem's chief virtues is discovered in its strictly controlled patterns of thought and rhythm. Colin shifts from grief to joy partly by means of his discursive rhetoric, partly by means of the control that his meter and rhyme exercise over our ears. The refrain especially, with its liturgically persistent repetition of the "verse/hearse" rhyme, suggests that the poem itself metaphorically resurrects Dido. Her progress from death to heavenly life is encompassed by the stately, quite visible movement of the stanzaic pattern, so that the highly organized rhythm and palpable form of the elegist's song indeed become the happy hearse of Dido's apotheosis. While it is certainly true that Colin's poem canot physically revive Dido or conquer the realities of death for any other mortal, his performance makes death more acceptable by placing it within a more broadly natural perspective. Colin asserts that death is not a perpetual darkness inflicted by the "dreaded sisters." On the contrary, death is an unburdening of mortality, a release into the "heauens hight" (176) of eternal bliss. Poetry cannot prevent death, but it can grant the poet a vision of its real meaning, a vision of Dido walking in the Elysian Fields, that the elegist has the power to transmit to his fellowman. His success, then, is twofold. We accept his instruction because we have been included by means of various poetic devices, in the imaginative act that discerns a meaningful connection between life and death. At the same time, we are convinced of the unimpeachable power of the poet's vision. Dido is not resurrected by the dear might of him who walked the waves, although there are suggestions of Christian redemption subdued beneath the pastoral veil. She is resurrected by the poet's realization that death has its own decorous place in the harmony of the universe. Dido's unbodied "blessed soule" (178), relieved of its "burdenous corpse" (166), exemplifies the continuum between life and death, whose outlines are susceptible to the poet's imaginative vision. It is characteristic of the orphic elegy that by the end of the performance death has been made meaningful and that we are left not with a sense of empty finality, but with a sense of completeness.

The full impact of the orphic quality of "November" becomes clear when it is set beside Spenser's adonean elegy, *Astrophel*. This later poem, probably modeled on Ronsard's *Adonis* and indirectly, Bion's *Lament for Adonis*, was published in the 1595 volume *Colin Clouts Come Home Againe*. Following *Astrophel* in the same volume is not only *The Lay of Clorinda*, but also five other elegies for Sidney by various hands. The *Lay* has offered problems about its authorship, since it purports to have been the work of Sidney's sister, the Countess of Pembroke, although it is now generally held to be by Spenser himself.[23] Because Spenser appended the *Lay* specifically to *Astrophel*, questions arise about the purpose of the appendage and the relation between the two parts of the poem. The *Lay*'s tone and mood diverge sharply from the narrative body of *Astrophel* in that it carries the burden of the classic lament-consolation formula missing from the main part of the poem. Clearly, though, we are meant to consider both parts of the poem as a whole, with the *Lay* reflecting back upon the narrative body, tempering its character by means of its traditional elegiac motifs.

In spite of the fact that *Astrophel* celebrates Philip Sidney, the poem itself does not lament the death of a poet, but rather the death of a soldier. Whether or not Spenser's model in Ronsard or even in Bion demanded that the subject of his elegy be an adventurer, it is still striking that there is but one allusion in the poem to Astrophel's role as a poet. It occurs almost casually, well into the narrative of the shepherd-soldier's life:

> Ne her with ydle words alone he wowed,
> And verses vaine (yet verses are not vaine)
> But with braue deeds to her sole seruice vowed,
> And bold atchieuements her did entertaine.
>
> [67-70]

The lines suggest that Astrophel's attachment to poetry, other than as an amatory pastime, was certainly subservient to his deeds of martial prowess. The elegist makes a parenthetical and, given the usual claims made for the poet's powers in the pastoral elegy, rather feeble defense of "verses vaine," one that hardly draws our attention away from the biography of Astrophel. But this is the nature of this poem. It is very much "about" its subject, the dead Astrophel, in a way that "November" was not "about" the dead Dido. We have a clear image of Astrophel, the courteous martial hero par excellence, far surpassing Spenser's portrait of Dido for particularity of detail. The earlier poem occasioned Colin Clout's skillful exercise to enunciate truths on the nature of life, death, and immortality. In *Astrophel* the elegist avoids these issues and concentrates on setting forth a pattern of manly perfection in the figure of his subject.

The business of the narrative body of the poem, then, is to glorify the dead shepherd-soldier at the expense of the speaker's own reflections on, say, the nature of his art. This is not true of the invocation, however. In the introductory three stanzas, printed in different type from the rest of the poem in the first edition, we hear a far different voice from that in the narrative proper.[24] In the early lines we hear the courtly Spenser assuming the rustic weeds:

Shepheards, that wont on pipes of oaten reed,
Oft times to plaine your loues concealed smart:
And with your piteous layes have learnd to breed
Compassion in a countrey lasses hart.
Hearken ye gentle shepheards to my song,
And place my dolefull plaint your plaints emong.

Here is a poet concerned with his craft, speaking to other poets. We would expect an orphic elegy to follow with a conventional *consolatio* at the end. That this is not in fact the case, that *Astrophel* proper closes without a consolation, raises the suspicion that the introductory stanzas were added, like the *Lay* itself, after the main body of the elegy had been composed. There simply is no integral place in the narrative for the kind of consolation that is issued in the *Lay*. Nor does the elevated and formal quality of the invocation correspond to the rustic tone of the narrative action. Both addenda reveal an uncertainty on the author's part in presenting for public perusal an elegy that has no consolatory conclusion.

The main section of the poem, like adonean elegies in general, verges on the nonpastoral. The eulogy for the dead Astrophel, as the elegist announces in his invocation, is intended to move his listeners "to pity such a case" (18). The pastoral conventions, then, are deployed with restraint, so as not to diminish the "pity" inherent in the situation, and the narrative closes with an expression of general woe:

And euery one did make exceeding mone,
With inward anguish and great grief opprest:
And euery one did weep and waile, and mone,
And meanes deviz'd to shew his sorrow best.
That from that houre since first on grassie greene,
Shepheards kept sheep, was not like mourning seen.
[205-10]

The hyperbole of every phrase of the passage indicates the elegist's technique. The pastoral garb is worn lightly; the last lines could be easily dismissed or translated into real-life terms. The transparency of the pastoral allegory allows the elegist to create an intimately lifelike situation, in which pastoral terms are clearly meant to correspond to the events of Sidney's life and death.

Another effect is also achieved, and this is manifested in the elegist's emotional attitude toward his subject. Far from assuming the detached, olympian air of Colin Clout in "November," Astrophel's elegist is highly involved with the matter of his poem.[25] His overwrought emotion prevails even in the final lines, where we would expect a calmer mood to appear. By simply piling up terms of bewailment ("exceeding mone," "anguish," "great grief," and so forth) and even by repeating the verb "mone" to rhyme with its nominal homonym, the elegist exposes his own unsettled, unsure, and personal reaction to the reality of Astrophel's death. He is not capable of consoling his listeners in the way that Dido's elegist could console and even preach to his audience. He explains why in a simple, direct couplet halfway through the poem:

> The dolfulst beare that ever man did see
> Was *Astrophel*, but dearest vnto mee.
>
> [149-50]

Like Virgil's speaker in *Eclogue* 10, he does not emphasize the intimacy of feeling behind his friendship with the subject of his elegy. It is in the backgrond, understated and poignant.

There are, in fact, strong resemblances between the Gallus *Eclogue* and Spenser's elegy for Sidney. Both Gallus and Astrophel were actual men, known to the respective audiences of Virgil and Spenser. In each poem we are given a glimpse of what purports to be a historical situation, grounded in the recognizable features of the poet's life and only half-filtered through the screen of the pastoral form. Both Gallus and Astrophel are soldiers; and although both are poets as well, it is the role of each as soldier that the elegist chooses to emphasize. The effect of such role-assigning draws attention not to the verse of the elegist, or to poetry in general, or to the ritual it may enact, but to the deeds, exploits, and valor of the dead hero himself. No substantial claim is made in either poem for the preservation of the dead man's memory within the verse of the elegist. Such a claim, while appropriate to, and effective in, an orphic elegy, would be out of place where only the barest consolation can be gleaned from the terrible shock of untimely death. Grief and finality are the emotions that adonean elegies present and distill.

Spenser's achievement in *Astrophel* lies in this very portrayal of grief. In spite of the regularity of the meter and the patterned *ababcc* rhyme scheme, many eruptions of parenthetical asides and appositive clauses convey the distress of the elegist at the events described. For example, after Astrophel is gored through the thigh like Adonis, neighboring shepherds rush to the bleeding hero:

> They stopt his wound (too late to stop it was)
> And in their armes then softly did him reare:
> Tho (as he wild) vnto his loued lasse,
> His dearest loue him dolefully did beare.
>
> [145-48]

The rush of events and the elegist's haste to describe all, while simultaneously editorializing, force the verse to tumble out as both narrative and commentary. At last he despairs of succeeding in his narrator's role and relies on a convenient *topos*:

> The rest of [Stella's] impatient regret,
> And piteous mone the which she for him made,
> No toong can tell, nor any forth can set,
> But he whose heart like sorrow did inuade.
>
> [169-72]

It would be difficult to forgive Spenser a line like "And

piteous mone the which she for him made," if it were not
necessary to remember that the shepherd elegist plays his rude
role well in the poem. The gusto with which he describes the
violence of Astrophel's death would not have sat at all com-
fortably in "November," where Colin provides none of the
details of Dido's end. But the adonean elegy achieves much
of its power in the violence of its emotion and the vividness of
the suffering it depicts. Spenser seizes the opportunity for this
kind of emotional violence in allowing his rustic elegist to
describe Astrophel's last stand with nothing short of ferocity:

> Eftsoones all heedlesse of his dearest hale,
> Full greedily into the heard he thrust:
> To slaughter them and worke their finall bale,
> Least that his toyle should of their troups be brust.
> Wide wounds emongst them many one he made,
> Now with his sharp borespear, now with his blade.
>
> . . . . . . . . . . . . . . . . . . . . . . . . . . . . . . . . . . . . . . . . . . . . . .
>
> So as he rag'd emongst that beastly rout,
> A cruell beast of most accursed brood
> Vpon him turnd (despeyre makes cowards stout)
> And with fell tooth accustomed to blood,
> Launched his thigh with so mischieuous might,
> That it both bone and muscles ryued quight.
>
> [103-120]

Had Spenser described Sidney's actual performance at Zut-
phen in these terms, he would have painted a picture of barbarism. But Astrophel's siege of the "beastly rout" is
justified under the auspices of both pastoral and the Adonis
story that it echoes. The elegist's rudeness, after all, makes
such descriptions acceptable. Here is no Colin Clout reaching
for his oaten reed at the first mention of death to intone
neoplatonic high seriousness. As a convincingly rustic
shepherd, Astrophel's elegist would be expected to speak
with force and simple conviction. His strong appeal to power-

ful emotions, his feelings of loss at Astrophel's death, befit his humble station; but the rigors of such a role rarely invite acceptable consolation in the elegy. One the other hand, Spenser's traditionalism is too powerful to omit all consolation, so the stricken elegist must make way for Astrophel's sister, Clorinda.

Even in itself, the *Lay* is not a successful elegy. Its movement from lamentation to consolation is unprepared for and unjustified. The mood changes from woe to joy, it seems, in the breath taken between two succeeding lines. After Clorinda has implored the heavens, cursed the fates, and apostrophized Death, she asks the crucial question that in the next line she answers for herself:

> Ay me, can so diuine a thing be dead?
> Ah no, it is not dead, ne can it die,
> But liues for aie, in blisfull Paradise.
>
> [66-68]

This forced attempt, however, cannot assuage her distress entirely. Although she claims that she must accept Astrophel's apotheosis, she concedes that we here below must "waile his priuate lack" (89). She concludes by addressing the dead soldier on high:

> But liue thou there still happie, happie spirit,
> And giue vs leaue thee here thus to lament:
> Not thee that doest thy heauens ioy inherit,
> But our owne selues that here in dole are drent.
> Thus do we weep and waile, and wear out eies,
> Mourning in others our owne miseries.
>
> [91-96]

What little consolation Spenser has given with one hand for the sake of propriety, he has taken back with the other for the sake of credibility. The emptiness of Clorinda's attempt to rejoice is finally matched only by the stereotyped mold from which her expression falls. A picture of Astrophel,

. . . compast all about with roses sweet,
And dainty violets from head to feet,

[71-72]

is cloying and faintly ludicrous when placed against the poem's earlier gallant portrait of him. When reading the *Lay* it is difficult not to recall Dr. Johnson's judgment of Congreve's pastoral elegies: when the author "has yelled out many syllables of senseless dolor, he dismisses his reader with senseless consolation."[26] Even had the dolor been fuller of sense, though, the change to consolation would have had to be more fully anticipated, emotionally, in order to be justified. As it is, the reader is buffeted by a display of grief that in no way prepares for its reversal.

The confusions of *Astrophel* are inherent in its point of view and typical of many adonean elegies. The harmonies of nature and the stasis of past time that are exploded by death are usually best repaired, in the orphic fashion, by a consummate act of the elegist's imagination. Like Colin Clout or the duo of *Eclogue* 5, the elegist can more easily transcend the chaos of the bereaved present by means of an imaginative assertion of his powers in reshaping and healing painful experience. His mediation between the world of death and loss and the world of beauty and timelessness convinces us only if he projects a confident, almost serene disposition. In short, if he wishes to console, he cannot feel bereavement to the extent that he is paralyzed with grief. *Astrophel* fails ultimately, if it is read with the *Lay* intact, because its structure is fragmented and its tone uneven. Spenser tries to make the poem something it cannot be. Both the invocation to *Astrophel* and the apotheosis in the *Lay* attempt a confident assertion that is betrayed by the distress that Astrophel's death has implacably left behind.

These strictures are confirmed when we consider a brilliant adonean elegy, the *Epitaphium Damonis*. Milton's Latin elegy, written to bewail the death of his close friend, Charles

Diodati, and perhaps the most personally intimate poem he wrote, remains solidly adonean even though it concludes in high orphic pitch. Thyrsis's attempt to apotheosize Damon in the final movement of the poem, it seems to me, neither convinces nor does justice to the poem as a whole. It is, nevertheless, a skillful maneuver that almost succeeds. The measure of its success lies in the poem's almost convincing shift from an outright adonean bewailment to a grand orphic celebration, a shift that is subtly prepared for'and intricately carried through. Milton's craftsmanship alone, however, cannot transform this beautiful personal lament into the prophetic and quite impersonal vision that the apotheosis proffers as the poem's *ratio operandi*. Milton saw that, if he wanted to add a Christian consolation to the poem on which it is modeled, the bleak, adonean *Alcon* of Castiglione,[27] more preparation for that consolation would have to be made than is to be found in, say, *The Lay of Clorinda*. The result is an ingenious attempt.

Recent critics of the poem, most illuminating of whom has been A. S. P. Woodhouse,[28] have defended it against earlier charges that the poem fails because it "reveals a troubled, disunited mind" that cannot resolve the painful experience of death.[29] Woodhouse bases his defense on the idea that the theme of immortality appears almost at the beginning in the pagan form of an immortality of remembrance (18-34). It appears tentatively again in the middle part of the poem, in a form that hints that for Damon death is not the end (123). Finally life triumphs over death with the ecstatic Christian upsurge in the concluding vision of the heavenly Damon. The turning point of the poem occurs in the passage describing the carved cups given by Manso to Thyrsis (179-97). As Woodhouse was the first to perceive, Milton has transformed this traditional gift-giving motif into a symbol of heaven and resurrection. The pictures of the Red Sea and the sky point to divine love, and the image of the Phoenix to renewal and rebirth, thereby symbolically propelling the elegist to his beatific vision. "It is to this conclusion," Woodhouse asserts, "that the pictures on the cups have been leading us unawares."

Woodhouse's observations are undeniably valid. Milton has gone to great lengths to ensure a triumphant conclusion that is symbolically prepared for in the course of the poem. The apotheosis lacks, however, an answer to the great problem that the poem continually reiterates: how is Thyrsis to be compensated for his loneliness now that Damon is dead? Thyrsis's piercing and insupportable solitude is the keynote of the poem. As we learn in the Argumentum, *se suamque solitudinem hoc carmine deplorat;* he bewailed himself and his loneliness in this song. The resonances of this theme are so powerful that even the orchestral conclusion cannot completely drown them out.

Thyrsis begins to stress his separation from the dead Damon in the invocation (1-18). Their separation began before Damon's death, while Thyrsis remained "in the Tuscan city," thereby depriving himself of even the small consolation of a final reunion before his friend's death. The agony of loneliness is insurmountable for Thyrsis, even when he consoles himself that Damon will be remembered in the hearts of men. *At mihi quid tandem fiet modo*, he cries, "But what at last is to become of me?" (37). This question is repeated almost laboriously in various forms for at least the next thirty lines (37-67). Each time he implores *Pectora cui credam* ("To whom shall I trust my heart?"), he chooses a different pastoral image to signify his loneliness; but the image he chooses separates quite easily from the emotion it is meant to express. For example:

> . . . quis me lenire docebit
> Mordaces curas, quis longam fallere noctem
> Dulcibus alloquiis, grato cum sibilat igni
> Molle pirum, et nucibus strepitat focus . . .?

Who will teach me to quiet gnawing cares, to beguile the long nights with sweet conversation, when the mellow pear hisses on the cheerful fire and the hearth crackles with nuts . . . ?

[45-48]

The lines are symptomatic of the adonean tendency that cannot integrate the pastoral conventions with the experience of grief. The results leaves a perilous gap between convention and emotion. In a similar way, Thyrsis's loneliness is never fully reconciled to the triumph dictated by the orphic conclusion.

Milton does, however, skillfully adapt a host of other pastoral conventions to the service of his main theme, loneliness and separation. The feeling of bitter resentment against fate for having taken a life in full bloom has been a standard feature of the pastoral elegy since at least Virgil's *Eclogue* 5.[30] By assigning this complaint to Thyrsis (19-20), Milton heightens the poignance of individual bereavement and stresses the suffering of one specific man. In the same way, the contrast between the immortality of nature and the mortality of man intensifies Thyrsis's alienation. In nature, he says, all animals are gregarious and without feeling for one another as individuals. When one of them dies, there are others to transfer affection toward. But men, "alien to one another and discordant in heart" (*aliena animis, et pectore discors*, 107) can scarcely find one among thousands. If a friend is lost, an undying hurt is left for all eternity (*aeternum linquens in saecula damnum*, 111). Thyrsis's utter and hopeless solitude is as profound and long-lasting as his humanity. The poem devolves further into inexorable grief as it accumulates new images and twists old conventions to deepen the loneliness of the mourner and the finality of death. The pathos of an adonean elegy, when as powerfully conceived as the *Epitaphium*, achieves its fullest expression in the bleakness of an empty future.

One section of the poem (111-179) consists of Thyrsis's

reminiscence of his Italian journey and his plans for a projected English epic. Whether or not Thyrsis's memories of Italy are justified by the total plan of the poem, an abiding sense of his separation from Damon maintains its hold on his imagination. He recalls how he had fondly thought of Damon as alive and happy in England, even after his friend had died. The irony of his misimpression increases his bitterness. Still, he says, he will rehearse his ambition to sing in heroic verse. Thyrsis now breaks into an exalted flight, in the tradition that sanctioned the elegist's account of his own poetic activities.

Although this passage can be read as an instrument for increasing the excitement as the poem begins to turn to its grand conclusion,[31] it is nevertheless gravely susceptible to the very charges of arrogance that the elegist fears (*dubito quoque ne sim/Turgidulus*, 159-60). The note is jarring and ill-conceived; it has caused Douglas Bush to complain that "we may for once find a touch of egotism, or at least a want of tact, in the elaboration of Milton's epic plans."[32] Had the poem been less adonean, had it exhibited less sorrow and personal bereavement throughout, then perhaps this touch of egotism would not have been inappropriate. After all, *Lycidas* exhibits a similar concern for the elegist's own poetic ambitions. The *Epitaphium*, however, presents itself on different terms. If the speaker's elaboration of his epic plans are intended to compensate somehow for the sense of loneliness that he has been building up through the poem, we can only be left a bit cold by it all. True enough, Milton makes the best of an impossible task by using the passage as a transition to the new note of triumph. This does open a different door to the future, where we are allowed to look at Thyrsis's projected poetry. But it still leaves the burden of Thyrsis's inexorable loneliness unrelieved; Damon will still be dead. In the concluding lines, Thyrsis invokes Damon to "stand graciously by me and serencly favor me" (*Dexter ades, placidusque fave*, 208); but this too is a very distant sort of kinship, and the hope is not congruent with the elegist's earlier fervor. We can accept Lycidas's role as the Genius of the shore, because no effort comparable to Thyrsis's has been made in that poem to heighten the personal bereavement of the speaker. To transform Damon into a patron saint, though, is to sacrifice the pathos of Thyrsis's earlier grief. The poem has fallen into two weakly related utterances; Damon's conventional apotheosis is not prepared by, and not strong enough to overcome, the anguish of the rest of the poem.

It may be tempting to exploit the shortcomings of the *Epitaphium* as a foil against which *Lycidas* may shine more brightly and win more hearts. To do so not only would rehearse a stale exercise in the obvious, but also would fall slightly beside the point. The two poems are kith, more than simply by virtue of their common genre. For while it would seem inevitable that we designate *Lycidas* immediately as the orphic elegy par excellence, it in fact incorporates, like the *Epitaphium*, the incentives and characteristics of both the adonean and the orphic strains. But whereas Milton disappoints us in the *Epitaphium* by forcibly grafting an orphic conclusion to an otherwise persistently adonean utterance of grief, he shapes *Lycidas* by tapping equally and consistently the resources of both strains. Within the poem Milton forges an intense imaginative dialectic between orphic ritual and adonean despair, between detached pastoral artifice and the distraught emotions attendant upon untimely death.[33] In spite of its progressive movement to a "higher mood" (87) and the joyous apotheotic vision intended to resolve all earlier contradictions and doubts, *Lycidas* does not finally resolve its tensions—aesthetically, emotionally, or otherwise. Nor am I convinced that it must be seen to do so in order to have earned its fame in the pantheon of English verse. Quite the contrary, I wish to offer the simple notion that *Lycidas* for all its aesthetic unity, is a distressing and discomfiting poem. Its power, its success lie in its utterly perfect balance between the orphic and adonean perspectives on death. This balance exerts its control over us so subtly that at the end of the elegy we are left—more often than we admit—perplexed and uncertain about the confrontation between a greatly gifted imagination and the universal enigmas of death, immortality, and the value of life. For this reason, even if it were not the consummate achievement of the elegiac tradition, *Lycidas* would continue to provoke a superabundance of commentary. Of course, like all great works of art, it is inexhaustible to repeated analysis and enjoyment. But more to the point, *Lycidas* captivates us because it profoundly disturbs and resists the critical faculty that seeks a comprehensible and comprehensive account of the poem's power to move us. Far from challenging the richly diverse and distinguished commentary that this century has devoted to the poem, I find myself in bewildering agreement with a host of instructive and ingenious analyses, many sharply contradictory of one another. This very diversity reflects—as *Hamlet* perhaps does—the poem's radically unsettling, distressing essence, a discrepancy between the orphic resolutions it asserts and the residue of doubt it leaves behind. Milton lures us into the belief that *Lycidas*, like the *Epitaphium*, can be probed by the critical intelligence in order to account for its triumphant conclusion. Keeping in mind the Latin elegy and the distinctions between the orphic and adonean responses, we may best approach the poem by observing how Milton masters both impulses, without, finally, sacrificing one to the other.

We are led directly into this monody in which "the Author bewails a learned Friend" by a speaker whose rather abrupt rhythms and rebellious anger portend an adonean lament of grief and confusion in the face of untimely death:

> Yet once more, O ye Laurels, and once more
> Ye Myrtles brown, with Ivy never sear,
> I com to pluck your Berries harsh and crude,
> And with forc'd fingers rude,
> Shatter your leaves before the mellowing year.

Bitter constraint, and sad occasion dear,
Compells me to disturb your season due:
For *Lycidas* is dead, dead ere his prime,
Young *Lycidas*, and hath not left his peer.

[1-9]

His elevated invocation to the emblematic plants does not fully compensate for the calming and distancing effect that would have been provided by a traditional prologue on the order of, say, *Eclogue* 5. Instead, this decidedly young elegist barely conceals the emotional violence that every individual undergoes when he is unwillingly "forc'd" to accept the response that death "compells" from him. He must "shatter" and "disturb" the natural order of the mellowing year in an act commensurate with his own desolation and shock as he confronts an unwarranted death.

From another, equally valid perspective, the elegist's opening lines balance our response to his personal grief by stimulating our recognition that his utterance resounds with the echoes of a literary mainstream that defies the expression of subjectively intimate mourning. His studied employment of the artificial niceties of the pastoral elegiac tradition mitigates, or tempers, our personal sympathy for him. Flourishing the literary emblems of laurel, myrtle, and ivy in his opening cadences, the elegist invites us to place him at the end of a classical tradition of (in M. H. Abrams's words) "public performance of ritual elegy."[34] These poetic berries, though harsh and crude, have felt many a poet's finger, forced and otherwise, before now. Without detracting from his expression of genuine pity, the poet universalizes his lament under the auspices of a literary tradition that distances and depersonalizes grief. Both elegiac strains—one for the calming literary ritual, the other for the grief-ravaged bewailment—do not merely balance one another: they contend with one another, as they will throughout the poem.

We can estimate the intricacy of this contention and the extent to which it pervades the poem by pausing over Milton's alternating manipulation of the poem's famous recurring images. To take one that has received its due of attention, the water imagery in the poem reflects the speaker's preoccupation with opposite primordial forces, which in the universal scheme of things cannot be reconciled.[35] The tranquil and sanctified Galilean lake figures forth in the speaker's mind as powerfully as his image of the remorseless deep that took Lycidas's life. Water in the poem functions not so much as an emblem of both life and death, but more accurately, as an emblem of *either* life *or* death, depending upon the particular mood and moment of its appearance in the speaker's meditation, upon the focus of his energies as he contemplates Lycidas's end. The power of his imagination is such that not even the vision of "the dear might of him that walk'd the waves" (173) can fully quell the fury of the "whelming tide" (157) that he envisions with equal fervor.

As an emblem of either life or death, water represents to the speaker a force analogous to that of his own poem. On one hand, he sheds a "melodious tear" to bewail Lycidas's death, but on the other, he intends his elegy to act as a balm, a "meed" (14) against the parching wind that abuses Lycidas's floating body. Recalling the "verse/hearse" rhyme of "November," we do not read the poem overliterally when we recognize that the elegist hopes that his poetic "tear" will become the "bier" of the aimlessly drifting bones of the dead youth. He sheds, then, a "melodious" tear, which, like Lycidas's lofty rhyme, requires skill and construction. Its seat is the "sacred well" (15) of the Muses, another image of containment that suggests redemptive possibilities. As an organizing and controlling agent, meant to harmonize and provide ritual meaning for Lycidas's death, the elegy must continually contend against the wild and discordant forces that have set Lycidas's body adrift. For this reason, both meanings provided by the O.E.D. of the word "hearse" have relevance: it is both a "bier; a coffin," and a "solemn obsequy in a funeral." The "Laureat Herse where *Lycid* lies" (151), summoned up late in the poem, refers to the elegist's own imaginative process as well as to any hearse he may picture. Both hearses, as it were, amount to a "false surmise" (153) when matched by the speaker's equally strong vision of Lycidas's body being hurled by the whelming tide.

It is important not to underestimate the elegist's preoccupation with the physical realities of both Lycidas's body and Lycidas's bier, because that preoccupation reflects the contending impulses of the opposing elegiac strains. The elegist's song, closely akin in his mind to the bier of the funeral ritual, partakes of the control and harmony that music generates throughout the poem. Like the water imagery, music has attracted the attention of nearly every reader. Anatomized in the rhythms and structure of the verse and repeated in numerous metaphors throughout the poem, music finds its most powerful embodiment in the elegist's awesome recollection of his bygone youth with Lycidas. The shepherd boys, together with the pastoral fauns and satyrs, "temper'd" (33) their rural ditties to the inaudible melodies of the spheric movements and sidereal regularity. [36] At the joyous apotheotic moment, the elegist once again hears these primordial melodies re-created anew, as Lycidas joins the "unexpressive nuptial Song" (176) of the heavenly choirs. The associative, cumulative impact of all of the suggestions and images clustering around the music of the poem—the bygone pastoral song, the elegist's melodious tear, the laureate hearse, the angelic harmonies—comprise an orphic bulwark against the equally powerful and disruptive forces of natural chaos. In a similar way, it is worth noting that the elegist contemplates, in proper orphic fashion, his own death with a literal image of containment:

> So May some gentle Muse
> With lucky words favour my destin'd Urn,
> And as he passes turn,

And bid fair peace to my sable shrowd.

[19-22]

The elegist envisions the continuous reenactment of literary mourning according to an almost instinctive association of the "lucky words" of some "gentle Muse" with his own funeral "Urn."

Whenever the elegist contemplates Lycidas's death from an adonean perspective, these images of harmony and containment are twisted to express the horror of the speaker's most intimate and fearful imaginings. Jolted by the shock that Lycidas is "gon, and never must return" (38) the elegist no longer hears the "glad sound" (35) of his boyhood, but instead the mournful echoes of "Woods, and desert Caves" (39). Without the harmonies of Lycidas's "soft layes" (44), the landscape is perceived as "wild" (40) and "killing" (45). These grim observations seem to give rise almost naturally to the Orpheus passage, which Milton skillfully manipulates as part of the convention that asks "Where were ye, Nymphs?" Rather than invoking Orpheus's name as a reminder of the powers of the poet to tame nature, however, the elegist pictures the primordial poet overpowered by the "rout that made the hideous roar" (61), his "gory visage" (62) wildly sliding down the swift Hebrus.[37] For a moment—in fact for the entire passage that questions the "homely slighted Shepherds trade"—the elegist gives voice to an adonean *cri de coeur* of personal frustration and unrestrained anxiety. The forces of chaos, present even in the "tangles" (69) of Neaera's hair, overwhelm the speaker, in the same way that he has imagined them to overwhelm and drown all forces of order, harmony, and civilization from Orpheus to Lycidas.

The poem proceeds by alternating almost frantically between adonean despair and orphic enlightenment. Though the elegist submits to a strain "of a higher mood " (87) and is again induced to resume the "Oat" (88) of his pastoral forebears, he quickly returns to the anguishing mood that tells him that Lycidas' only bier

> . . . was that fatal and perfidious Bark
> Built in th' eclipse, and rigg'd with curses dark.
>
> [100-101]

Once again, astronomical and musical emblems of order have been yoked, but this time perverted, as heaven's eye is eclipsed and shepherd's song becomes "curses dark." The speaker's vision of experience has degenerated to the point where all that he has known of past harmony and meaningful serenity has been twisted into contrary, hellish, and wasteful shapes. As he contemplates a larger pattern of experience and considers Lycidas's now lost priestly aspirations, the voice of St. Peter issues a grim excoriation of corruption and fleshly servitude. The primal emblem of harmonious music is again summoned to show its perversion in the "Blind mouthes" (119) of corrupt priests. "Their lean and flashy songs/Grate on their scrannel Pipes of wretched straw" (123-24) and serve only to swell their sheep with wind and rank mist. Like Lycidas's dead body, threatened by the parching wind and in need of the elegist's melodious tear, the body of the church is now subject to the evil wind of a corrupt priesthood.

The violence of St. Peter's threat seems momentarily to calm the speaker, as he bids the Sicilian Muse of his literary ritual to return. The following culminating double vision of the flower catalogue and then of the sounding seas perfectly captures the pitch and toss of the speaker's imagination between orphic detachment and adonean horror. The flower passage allows the elegist to exercise with unmatchable virtuosity the strength of his imagination to retrieve Lycidas's body, to strew the dead youth's hearse with the flowers of his verse. The attempt is not unlike Colin Clout's depiction of Dido's body "on the beare when it was brought" (161). But whereas Colin's image of Dido's dead body impels his insight that she has now been happily "unbodied" and unburdened,

Milton's elegist is provided no such orphic comfort. His imagination operates precariously close to the disruptions and intrusions of subjective grief. He realizes, with adonean pathos, that his imagination cannot retrieve Lycidas, that his "frail thoughts dally with false surmise."

The sounding seas where the speaker is now led present the terrible images, common to the adonean lament, of the actual mutilated body of the dead hero. Lycidas's bones, far from being contained within the hearse of the elegist's ritual elegy, are hurled in a monstrous world where no sheep graze and no satyrs dance. The very geographical range of the speaker's vision in this passage, akin to the range of Damon's and Astrophel's elegists, dissipates the efficacy of the poet's power to depict the dead shepherd's redemption. The import of his vision stresses that he cannot, unaided and through his own imagination, provide the meed that will save Lycidas from the parching wind and the sea of death.

There are numerous ingenious and plausible explanations of the speaker's sudden realization that Lycidas is not dead. His shift from woe to joy, according to Abrams's judicious account, for example, is reached "by a gradual shift from the natural, pastoral, and pagan viewpoint to the viewpoint of Christian revelation and its promise of another world, the Kingdom of Heaven."[38] Other readings have reinforced this interpretation by examining the various resurrection myths associated with dolphins in pagan literature,[39] or by assigning a primary redemptive role to St. Michael, who looks at Lycidas's body and melts with ruth.[40] William Madsen has proposed that "the consolation passage is spoken by another voice, perhaps that of the archangel Michael, the guardian of the Mount"[41]; and a recent explanation also attempts to explain the transition in terms of a deliberate change of "voices."[42] Most of these accounts assume that Milton's ways can be justified, by one critical means or another. With this ideal I concur, but it seems at least possible that the poem's sudden shift from its emotional nadir to its apotheotic climax

constitutes a form of unity in itself, based on the tension between the orphic and adonean responses to death. The final
transition from woe to joy most strenuously exerts the unify-
ing dialectic that has pervaded the poem until now. Both
polarities continue to exert their pressure even through the
conclusion, defying our attempts to comprehend the
speaker's "resolution" of his meditative process.

Lycidas's apotheosis, echoing so strongly the Book of
Revelation and the commonplaces of pastoral, does of course
fulfill the elegist's repeated exertions to comprehend
Lycidas's death. The swain's earthly song now submits to the
heavenly hymn of love; adonean grief is banished because the
speaker's "melodious tear" has been found only preliminary
to the "unexpressive nuptial Song" of the "sweet Societies"
(179) above. Yet even in the elegist's vision of the heavenly
Lycidas, we may detect an unwillingness to abandon
altogether the personal anxieties and grief that vie with the
progressively uplifting ritual in the rest of the poem. Isabel
MacCaffrey has observed that Milton's unusual use of a
simile in "this pervasively metaphorical poem" to describe
Lycidas's resurrection—"So sinks the day-star in the Ocean
bed . . . So *Lycidas* sunk low, but mounted high"
(168-72)—reassures us of the congruence between nature's
cycle and man's: "Milton wishes us to hold apart in imagination the various realms of being—natural, human, supernatural—precisely so that we can admire the marvelous
correspondences among them. . . In this new perspective of
analogy, 'nature' is seen to possess a metaphorical relevance
to human concerns."[43] This is an undeniably valid understanding of the function of Milton's simile; but it does not account for the studied contrivance inherent in the very choice
of the trope. By overtly comparing Lycidas to the sun, the
elegist *asserts* the authenticity of his vision, after the fashion
of a rhetorical prepositon. His assertion relies for its efficacy
upon the reader's recognition of an empirical phenomenon.
The simile must give us pause—literally—however fully we as-

sent to its emotional tenor. Though perfectly counterbalanced by the simplicity and beauty of the elegist's vision, this pause forces us to recall that, as Mrs. MacCaffrey seems to imply, for all his reassuring spiritual bliss, Lycidas has not surrendered his humanity, and therefore he must be mourned.

Because Lycidas never loses his humanity, as Dido must be said to have lost hers, he never altogether achieves the impersonality necessary to the orphic ritual. When Colin translates Dido to the heavens, he literally unbodies her: "She hath the bonds broke of eternall night/Her soule vnbodied of the burdenous corpse" (165-66). Though Lycidas's soul is "mounted high," we are not allowed to forget that his corpse is still "sunk low." The elegist's preoccupation with the actual body of the drowned youth haunts him, however subliminally, even in his ecstatic apotheotic vision of Lycidas's spiritual redemption. And although the elegist's poetry of Revelation assures us of Lycidas's joy, he would be hard put to assert flatly, with Dido's elegist:

> We deeme of Death as doome of ill desert:
> But knewe we fooles, what it vs brings vntil,
> Dye would we dayly once it to expert.
>
> [184-86]

Milton refuses to allow us to forget that he has written a monody to "bewail" Edward King, whatever his poetic obligations to seek and provide orphic consolation within the central affirmations of Christian faith.

The epilogue to the poem confirms its dual allegiance to the orphic and adonean response to death. That the ten-line conclusion continues to intrigue readers, who in turn continue to offer explanations of its function, suggests the possibility that Milton wrote the epilogue deliberately to bewilder his reader, that is, to force his reader to puzzle out the meaning not only of the epilogue, but also, in retrospect, of the elegy as an imaginative statement. After all, such a blatantly ambiguous conclusion is rare in Milton's poetry, and it is certainly uncharacteristic of him to leave us with so many contradictory critical options at such an important point. On one hand, we may legitimately regard the uncouth swain as the speaker of the elegy and therefore evaluate his transformation from the opening lines to the end of his song. His thought is now eager. Having been granted a vision of the heavenly host through the agency of his Doric quill, he may turn to new vistas with renewed hope. Or we may with equal plausibility conjecture that the epilogue reveals Milton's affirmation of the pastoral medium, tempered by Christian revelation, as a vehicle of imaginative truth. We may even validly choose to detect Milton's rejection of the pastoral mode, a rejection based on his realization that, unaided by divine revelation, he has proved imaginatively impotent to redeem Lycidas. This particular reading would help to explain the subdued mood of the speaker, for whom the gray morn and dropping sun sadly confirm his own eventual bodily extinction. The point is that Milton leaves open to our imaginations a variety of responses to the epilogue, all of which temper our responses to his elegy. The epilogue serves to remind us, in any event, that we cannot ignore the reality of natural life, and hence the inevitability of natural death. Above all, the epilogue persuades us that even a transcendent vision of Lycidas above cannot erase the pain, nor explain the mystery, of death. The elegist's vision, though, is neither undermined nor devalued by these grim realizations: rather, it is placed in a context of the larger patterns of spiritual renewal and hope.

*Lycidas* triumphs precisely because of its fidelity to *both* the adonean and the orphic responses to death. We respond to the experience of death with the elegist, at once intimately and ritually. Milton's refusal to provide a more comfortable answer—either adonean or orphic—to the universal mystery he confronts confers upon his poem its greatest glory. As we shall see in the following chapter, Milton's honesty, his refusal to provide us with easy solutions to difficult questions, is shared by Spenser in his allegory of the patterns of life and death in the pastoral world. The moral and aesthetic authenticity of both poets in their most intriguing pastoral poems is fostered, perhaps even directly maintained, by their mutual response to pastoral poetry. The detached intimacy of the mode allows the poet not only the means of grappling with his own vocational life, but also it provides the poet a unique means of drawing his reader into the arena of his imagination, to confront within the zodiac of the poet's wit the enigmas and burdens that befall our lives.

# 5

## Poet and Hero in Book 6 of *The Faerie Queene*

*T**he* trial of true courtesy in book 6 of *The Faerie Queene* embodies Spenser's most complete and perplexing treatment of the poetic imagination. Complete, because Spenser scrutinizes many facets of the life of the poet and the poet's place in society; perplexing, because he stubbornly refuses to provide easy solutions to the problems his narrative raises. He gives little quarter to those human and aesthetic impulses that demand an orderly explanation for life's dilemmas. On the contrary, he unsettles his readers and dislocates expectations of what the sixth book of *The Faerie Queene* ought to be about. Far from spoiling the book, however, the disorientation and uncertainty that are the hallmarks of this last completed segment of the poem confer on book 6 its chief glory as an artistic success.

Spenser chooses a pastoral setting for the core of book 6 as though this were the unquestionable way to go about writing the legend of courtesy. If we recall that pastoral by this time in Spenser's career has become the forum of the imagination, the green world that is itself a continued allegory for the poet's private inner world, we realize what attributes poetry shares with courtesy. Neither poetry nor courtesy can ever be completely at home in the court and the world of action. Yet outside of the social domain of the court, neither poetry nor courtesy carries moral influence powerful enough to justify its existence. What is the point of poetry or courtesy (as opposed to the less specifically *social* virtues of holiness, say, or temperance) if other men are not its benefactors? Civilized men acting in communities need both poetry and courtesy, according to Spenser's peculiar conception of them as moral activities, that is, as guides to humane and social life.

To invoke terms such as "moral" and "humane" in speaking of book 6 can be misleading, however, if one means only that Spenser's aim is to fashion a gentleman in virtuous and gentle discipline, as the poet himself states his intention in the letter to Raleigh.[1] Whatever moral program motivated the writing of *The Faerie Queene*, the poem's local intention is subsumed by the vision which deepens its meaning. In none of the books of the poem is an understanding of the overarching vision of life that consistently motivates the narrative more important than in book 6. The vagaries of criticism that surround the book testify to the difficulties readers have had in deriving from it a moral or even an aesthetic schema. Perhaps Spenser himself had difficulty in deciding how to define courtesy, or how to present his hero, or even how to end the book. The very insecurities that every reader feels when confronted by the uncomfortable and untidy particulars of book 6, however, constitute per se an imposing statement about the view of life that the book decidedly proffers. Summed up as a preamble to sharper consideration, that view comprehends human life as a deeply insecure affair, as often as not refusing to be shaped and organized into coherent patterns. Heroes disappear never to return, quests and aims fail with alarming regularity, and even a moment of seemingly mystical understanding cannot guarantee a tidy conclusion to the human drama. And yet heroes and poets must and will continue to quest. Spenser's conclusion, if we can call the end of this book a conclusion, says that poetry and courtesy, two of man's highest measures of his civilized status, give meaning to his life simply when he exercises his ability to practice them as disciplines.

Although these introductory remarks may seem to belie the point, it is of course the case that book 6 thrives because it is a narrative adventure inhabited by interesting characters. This is a story about flesh-and-blood humanity, from Briana and Crudor to Claribell and Bellamoure. A comprehensive understanding, then, must account first of all for Spenser's insistence that here before us lies a journey. The process itself, both of following the quest and of writing the poem, demands our interest and evaluation. This means that the object of Calidore's quest assumes less significance in the total conception than the local habitation and individual incident that he encounters along the way. In a parallel fashion, the poet's opening words ("The waies, through which my weary steps I guyde") alert us to the concern of this book for the tortuous paths of its own development. While one adventure leads sometimes quite logically to the next, more often than not the architectonically minded reader is forced to invent a comfortable structure on behalf of the book. This observation is not intended to deny the harmony of the book, but simply to assert that its unity and artistic wholeness derive from its view of human experience and from minute particulars of language and incident which reflect that view, rather than from its structure. The substitution of Calepine for Calidore in the middle cantos, for example, on the motive for which critics have exercised their ingenuity not altogether fruitlessly, at least confirms Spenser's refusal to be bound to a single hero or to one quest. To put the matter more positively, the Calepine cantos underline the joy of the book in the "sweet variety/Of all that pleasant is to eare or eye" (Proem 1), or what Kathleen Williams has called the "delight and liberty" of book 6.[2]

While delight and liberty are indeed keywords of the legend

of courtesy, they characterize only part of its spirit. An equally notable shroud of pessimism envelops the narrative, affecting virtually every incident. The conclusion, though hardly the only instance, comes to mind most readily. Perhaps an eagerness to look for a future with Providence as our guide would allow us to sweeten the bitterness of the conclusion or to ignore Calidore's inability to subdue the Blattant Beast permanently. Ameliorating responses of this sort are not altogether wrong, though they certainly distort the facts. The conclusion does not tell the whole story any more than the pastoral cantos do. To decide on categories such as "optimism" and "pessimism" as characteristic of the entire book is to ignore the seminal quality of all of Spenser's poetry: equilibrium, the reconciliation of opposite qualities.[3]

As many critics have labored to show in recent years, most notably Paul Alpers, Spenser's ability to induce moral understanding rather than moral judgment, gives color and shape to his poetry.[4] They have debated, for example, the vexing problem of Calidore's truancy in the pastoral world, with the result that it is generally agreed that a judicious viewpoint embraces the ambivalence of the issue.[5] The poet simultaneously condemns and commends Calidore for his truancy; the knight is guilty of ignoring his quest, but at the same time he is justified in his desire to remain in the pastoral environment. What is true of this example is true of the book as a whole, seen from a distance; Spenser's attitudes are balanced and exploratory. Urgent responsibilities to a corrupt court that harbors him compel not only Calidore, but certainly the poet-narrator as well. And yet that court, revolving around the glorious personage of the Queen, outshines any other in its virtue and courtesy. Both poet and hero clearly need a vision that supersedes and in some sense explains daily life; but just as clearly, they also belong in the imperfect court that has spawned them. Spenser's attempt to balance contending perspectives of this sort does not really lead him to a "poetry of reconciliation," as one critic maintains, but more properly to a poetry of the profoundest ambivalence.[6] The distinction is important. Spenser never tries to reconcile, for example, the "delight and liberty" of the book with the pessimism of the ending or the fear of the Beast. The cynicism and delight of book 6, like the good and evil in Milton's quotable remarks on our sage and serious Spenser, grow up together almost inseparably. In its various emblems and situations book 6 presents mutually inclusive views of man both in his fallen, death-bound state and in his capacity to persist and triumph over his frailty.

We have seen that a remarkably similar perspective animates *Lycidas* and Milton's early poetry in general; it is now helpful to recall the seasonal framework of the *Calender* to appreciate the full impact of Spenser's ambivalence. On one hand, the progress from "Januarye" to "December" testifies to the painful disparity between nature that renews itself cyclically and man who unrelentingly decays. The simple shepherd boy who plains his love in "Januarye" still pines in "December," and yet over the seasons his face has grown furrowed as he prepares to die. Though he has sprung from nature's bosom, individual man does not share her secret of endless renovation. His awareness of mortality, in fact, is accentuated by his very ties to the ever-regenerating landscape.

These depressing facts of life, however, are offset in the *Calender* by a strong sense of the human capacity to transcend mortality. Most readers have apprehended the paradox that the *Calender*'s affirmation of man's immortality is born in his apprehension of the transcendence within nature, the very forces that also provoke in him the burdens of mortality. "November" and "Aprill" herald the poem's most memorable assertions of life over death. Even though the celebration of Eliza and the apotheosis of Dido cannot negate mortality or even save Colin from despair, the poem's distinct affirmations of man's ties to an unchanging reality diminish the impact of his inevitable extinction. His capacity to discover something eternal and ever-reaching within himself offsets his obligation to death.[7]

Spenser's manipulation of pastoral to highlight man's mortality constitutes part of his success in revitalizing the form. In fact, Shakespeare's romances by a quite different route head toward the same goal: a perspective on life that in some sense heals the wound of human aging and mortality. The pastoral themes that invite a comparison between book 6 and the late Shakespeare share a preoccupation with the chronologial spectrum of life from youth to old age. The famous time-gap in *The Winter's Tale*, for example, startles the audience into a recognition that men indeed grow old and lose vitality. In a similar way, the narrative form of *The Faerie Queene* allows the poet to show us how men age and decay. Because the narrative poet has access to his characters' entire life histories, his outline of any individual's past and future provides a quite graphic demonstration of the aging process.

We have only to recall the older generation, most notably the hermit and Meliboe, to verify the significance of advanced age in this book. Of the hermit we are told that "[s]o long as age enabled him thereto" he strove after martial glory. "But being aged now and weary to/Of warres delight," he has retired to the "greene boughes, and flowers gay" of his hermitage (5. 37-38). However sage his abnegation of worldly strife, no gain can eradicate his proximity to death. Much the same is true of Meliboe, whose demise we actually witness. While some readers have found it painful to accept his violent death at the hands of the Brigants, there is only a slight attempt in the narrative to mourn his loss, chiefly because his advanced years have figured in Spenser's portrayal of him. The old man himself has stressed the gap that separates his "first prime of years" from his present idyllic old age, so that his death, even if it had not been an explicit narrative detail, has from the start been anticipated.

Many critics have pointed out that this is a book of youth. That observation must be qualified, however, to stress that its "youthful" quality depends to a large degree on the attention paid to the contrast between youth and age. Spenser's unusual emphasis on the emotional as well as the chronological bifurcation between the generations ought to be explored seriously, because the gap separating parent and child in the book comprises an important aspect of the poem's meaning. Young and old live in a perpetual state of tension that can never be wholly relieved. Frequently, moreover, our comprehension of an individual event in the narrative depends upon a recognition that various complexities arise from the relations between parent and child. It is essential, for example, that we be aware of Tristram as a foundling, and even more to the point, that this situation is the result of the "Untimely" (and therefore unnatural) death of his father, good King Meliogras. Or to choose an example more pertinent to the operations of courteous behavior, Priscilla and Aladine in their distress both return to the homes of their respective fathers. Aldus, the father of Aladine and a forerunner of the courteous old hermit, is one of the book's models of humane behavior, and his very name signifies his status as an elder. In the process of growing old, he has exercised remarkable courtesy, which the poet tells us was mastered in youth. The poet nonetheless takes the trouble to point out that not even a well-spent life exempts a man from the ravages of physical decay:

> He was to weete a man of full ripe yeares,
> That in his youth had beene of mickle might,
> And borne great sway in armes against his peares:
> But now weake age had dimd his candle light.
>
> [3.3]

One day, these words should remind us, the son's candle, and for that matter Calidore's as well, will dim like the father's.

The same episode presents a quite different parent in the person of Priscilla's dreadful father, whose wrath over his daughter's pursuit of her own heart everyone, including

Calidore, anticipates before the fact. Our awareness of Aldus's genuine love for his son enhances the other father's reputation as an autocratic parent of the nastiest sort. This awareness also affects Calidore to the extent that the lovers' account of the old man's refusal to permit their union prompts Calidore to his first explicit lapse. The young knight of courtesy places enough a priori faith in the certainty of the old man's ire to "giue faire colour" to Priscilla's story by transforming the truth into a "counter-cast of slight" (3.16-17). In such a way Spenser encourages us to conclude that one of the inescapable evils of the age barrier between young and old can often be a basis for distrust, unease, and discourtesy.

In a later episode Calidore again fails to deal courteously with an elder, this time in his notorious encounter with the ancient Meliboe. Whether the old man speaks genuinely and affirmatively for the joys attendant upon pastoral retirement, or whether he casts doubt on the very values he endorses by a tiresome display of prattle, remains suggestively (and perhaps intentionally) unclear. In either case, Calidore's social lapse in offering Meliboe gold in return for courteous hospitality derives at least partly from an inability to understand an older generation. The details of the incident bear this observation out. Not only does Meliboe himself make a great issue of his advanced years and his long-gone youthful experience, but both Calidore and the reader are aware that this is the father of Pastorella speaking. The young knight begins their conversation by addressing Meliboe as "ye father" (9.19), an appropriate cognomen, given Calidore's diverted attention during the conversation to the "real obiect of his vew" (9.26), his host's daughter. Calidore's effort to "insinuate his harts desire" (9.27) by ingratiating himself with the father of Pastorella, then, looms large in the young knight's obtuse disregard of his host's dicta. Once again, an underlying preoccupation with the effects and complexities of the human aging process works to color our understanding of courtesy as it is displayed in the minutiae of human intercourse.

The book's final assessment of the age difference that makes life difficult plays an important part in the resolution of one line of the narrative. Before Pastorella is reunited with her long-lost parents, Claribell and Bellamoure, the poet provides his readers with the details of their history. The opposition of Claribell's father to her union with Bellamoure (who, it should be noted, "whylome was in his youthes freshest flowre/a lusty knight," 12.3) led to their imprisonment and their subsequent loss of Pastorella. Only the old man's death releases the lovers, and it is not until they too have grown old that they are reunited with their daughter.

The restoration of the daughter to the parents also offsets the stress on the process of growing old by a compensating emphasis on rejuvenation. Just as youth inevitably implies eventual death, so too old age and death just as naturally imply rebirth, at least in terms of the species. Yet critics have noted that Pastorella "dies" in the Brigants' cave only to be reborn like the flower that is her emblem.[8] This remark holds true at every stage in book 6, as if to prove the continual reenactment of the laws of natural existence. A vivid example is presented by Calepine's encounter with Matilde, to whom he bequeaths the Bloody Babe. Matilde's misery resides in the prospect of her and Sir Bruin's dying without an heir:

> For th' heauens enuying our prosperitie,
> Haue not vouchsaft to graunt vnto vs twaine
> The gladfull blessing of posteritie,
> Which we might see after our selues remaine
> In th' heritage of our vnhappie paine:
> So that for want of heires it to defend,
> All is in time like to returne againe
> To that foule feend, who dayly doth attend
> To leape into the same after our liues end.
>
> [4.31]

Matilde grieves not for her own or her husband's ineluctable extinction, but for their want of what she envisions as a defense against "that foule feend" that threatens to consume all life. Calepine's gift of the foundling babe is the happiest of solutions, because for Matilde and Bruin, the babe is the gift of life. The poet acknowledges the success of Calepine's deed by looking ahead, in a revealingly characteristic way, to the babe's manhood:

> And it in goodly thewes so well vpbrought,
> That it became a famous Knight well knowne
> And did right noble deeds, the which elswhere are
>     showne.
>
> [4.38]

And so while the process of decay and death sets its mark on many of the characters, Spenser balances this unpleasant inevitability with an equal insistence on regeneration and a conviction in the heartiness of life to renew itself. The individual plight is marked by death; the species by continuous rebirth. Though human mortality is not negated in book 6, is is at least matched by a larger glimpse of man's participation in the eternal laws of renewal. If such remarks smack of a stiffly philosophical overview, one can only further admire Spenser's genius in making ideas poetry.

The wound inflicted by the Blattant Beast affords a suggestion about how life is renewed. While its insidious bite does not actually extinguish life, its victim is nevertheless incapacitated to the point of illness. The Hermit counsels the Squire and Serena that they must cure their physical wounds inflicted by the iron tooth of the beast by means of disicpline and virtue, through a spiritual renovation. Their restoration from illness to a renewal of life affirms the human capacity, which is both spiritual and self-generating, to overcome the forces of debilitation. Spenser's insistence on the triumph over death and degeneration is not, it must therefore be said, entirely a product of a mere acknowledgment that man procreates the race. Clearly man's ties with the generative processes of nature, an intimacy that resides at the heart of the pastoral view of life, complement his more powerful internal capacity to resist the forces of death. Pastorella's will to live, for example, sees her out of the Brigants' cave. Years earlier Bellamoure and Claribell displayed a similar resistance in their deathly dungeon. The poet does not know whether it was "through grace/Or secret guifts so with his keepers wrought" (12.6) that Bellamoure succeeded in finding his way to his wife in that dark cell. In either event, as a result of their inner strength, the seed of love was conceived in Claribell's womb to blossom forth miraculously in the restoration of Pastorella a generation later. "And liuest thou my daughter now againe," rejoices Claribell, "And art thou yet aliue, whom dead I long did faine?" (12.19)

The ambivalent movement between life and death that awes Claribell and that I am suggesting as the predominant quality of book 6 helps to make the flower its most appropriate and richly suggestive image.[9] Nearly every youth in the book is somehow associated with this simple image: in Calidore, gentleness and manners "were planted natural" (1.2); Tristram grew "like as flowre . . . shut vp in the bud from heauens vew" (2.35); Pastorella carries a flowermark on her breast. Even Mirabella, a lily that festered, had once been endowed with the "flowre/Of beauty" (8.20). All these blossoming young people flourish with the freshness that the image suggests.

Youth turns to age, though; flowers wither and die: this process is integral to an image that captures both sides of the peculiar perspective of the Book. When we are told, for example, that both Bellamoure and Meliboe blossomed in youth like flowers, the impact of human decay falls hard. As death advances relentlessly, flowers lose their bloom.

The pastoral framework that readily suggests the force of the flower as an emblem of life's transitory aspect also suggests the flower as an emblem of life's renewal as part of the seasonal rotation. Two seemingly contradictory yet really complementary processes, then, are endowed with poetic life by this image. Balancing the inevitability of human decline, Spenser continually reminds us of the perpetual reblossoming of youth in this book. The merely procreative is transcended once again by investing the pastoral metaphor of seasonal renewal with the spiritual quality that differentiates man from the rest of nature. To choose two paramount examples, Calepine recovers ("was woxen strong," 4.17) from the wound of the beast by means of an inner strength similar to that which allows Pastorella to survive the brutality of the Brigants.

As every reader of *The Faerie Queene* knows, the first and most memorable flower of book 6 is the "bloosme of comely courtesie" (Proem,5) that spreads itself through all civility. Spenser unifies the Legend of Courtesy by investing the flower with multiple meanings that spread themselves, it could be said, through all the book. Much more complex than a pastoral image of the cycles of life, the flower image acquires various nuances as it gradually illuminates, through reiteration and changing context, both courtesy and the poetic endeavor of writing about courtesy. The self-reflective aspect of the flower image, and indeed of the whole legend, is present from the proem onward. It is here, right at the beginning, that the poet establishes his intention to write not only about courtesy but also about poetry. This book will be the poet's legend too; it is he who will accompany Calidore on a double quest. Guiding his weary steps through the delightful land of Faery, he implores the Muses to grant him a vision that only they can achieve:

> Reuele to me the sacred noursery
> Of vertue, which with you doth there remaine,
> Where it in siluer bowre does hidden ly
> Since it at first was by the Gods with paine
> Planted in earth, being deriu'd at furst
> From heauenly seedes of bounty soueraine,
> And by them long with carefull labour nurst,

Till it to ripenesse grew, and forth to honour burst.

Amongst them all growes not a fayrer flowre,
Then is the bloosme of comely courtesie,
Which though it on a lowly stalke doe bowre,
Yet brancheth forth in braue nobilitie,
And spreds it selfe through all ciuilitie:
Of which though present age does plenteous seeme,
Yet being matcht with plaine Antiquitie,
Ye will them all but fayned showes esteeme,
Which carry colours faire, that feeble eies misdeeme.

[Proem, 3-4]

Spenser's tropes often demand almost overly detailed attention, which, while possibly subverting a degree of subliminal impact at first, tends to be useful in later readings. The proems of *The Faerie Queene* are especially susceptible to the scrutiny of the critical microscope because of their poetic density and because they often seem the clearest statements of the poet's intentions. The proem to book 6 assumes unusual significance by rehearsing in small compass the rhythms and patterns of the vision of life that the book as a whole will present.

The poet conceives of virtue as a sacred nursery planted *a principio* and tended by the gods until it "forth to honour burst." Like the other flowers of book 6, virtue has enjoyed its blossoming hour before succumbing to the unavoidable laws of decay. Unfortunately for the latter age, though, comely courtesy, one of virtue's fairest flowers, flourished in "plaine Antiquitie" and now retains only a deteriorated semblance of its pristine glory. The process of flourishing and decay is presented in the proem almost immediately; we may therefore expect that before its conclusion the poet will adumbrate the next stage of the cycle in a gesture of spiritual rebirth and rejuvenation.

First, though, it should be noted that the poet carefully distinguishes courtesy from virtue. Courtesy is only one of the flowers in the nursery of virtue, the flower that spreads itself through civility, while virtue itself lies hidden. The distinction is highly significant in an evaluation of courtesy as one of the glories of civilized man. A confusion between courtesy, as one of Spenser's famous "twelue priuate morall vertues," and virtue itself, as it is manifested in this book, must be rigorously avoided. Only, in fact, on Acidale will the implications of the distinction be revealed.

In the proem, at least, the flower image approximates the pattern that will become familiar through the narrative: the flowers of courtesy blossom to honor, only to wither with the passing years. The poet's lament for the fallen world of the present leads him to condemn those who are dazzled by contemporary, debased courtesy which is "now so farre from that, which then it was/That it indeed is nought but forgerie" (Proem,5). His deceived contemporaries, guilty chiefly of misperception, see only with their "feeble eies" and lack the inner vision necessary to distinguish between modern courtesy and its flourishing antique original.

The poet's characterization of his bedazzled contemporaries, their eyes fixed upon the blinding metallic speciousness that passes for genuine courtesy, contrasts with his own fervent poetic aspiration. While the eyes of even the wisest of his contemporaries can mistake brass for' gold, he himself asks a quite different kind of vision of the Muses. By an act of "infus[ion]" they "reuele" a vision in "the mindes of mortall men" that penetrates more deeply than mere visual sight to the source of "secret comfort, and . . . heuenly pleasure" (Proem,2). This infusion by which the Muses inspire, like the planting of virtue by the gods, will eventually well up and blossom in the mind of the poet. The flower metaphor makes intimate the relationship between the flourishing of virtue in antiquity and the flourishing imagination of the poet. Antique virtue and the poet's inner life, both actuated by supernatural agency, share an initial downward movement, which is in some sense hidden, and a subsequent growth and upward movement. Both eventually burst forth to honor.

The flower of the poet's imagination, the very poem that he asks for aid to write, illustrates the sense of process that inundates the book's perspective on life. Often this awareness of the poem as a process takes the form of the poet's familiar allusions to his work as a journey, especially as a sea voyage.[10] Perhaps the most interesting reference occurs in the opening stanza of canto 9, when after following Calepine through the middle episodes, the poet resumes his more comfortable role as the narrator of Calidore's quest:

> Now turne againe my teme thou jolly swayne,
> Backe to the furrow which I lately left;
> I lately left a furrow, one or twayne,
> Vnplough'd, the which my coulter hath not cleft:
> Yet seem'd the soyle both fayre and frutefull eft,
> As I it past, that were too great a shame,
> That so rich frute should be from vs bereft;
>
> [9.1]

The pose as a ploughman confers authority upon the poet and his poem, not only because of the literary association of the ploughman, but also because such a pose recalls and reencts the planting of virtue by the gods. By driving his plough down into the earth, the poet will cultivate the "rich frute" of which the world would otherwise remain bereft.

It follows, then, that the poem itself, like virtue, must in some sense grow, blossom, and decay. It is not, I think stretching Spenser's flexible design too far to apprehend the flower, in addition to its other meanings, as an image of the poem as it is actually being created. The dual movement toward both blossom and decay that characterizes the course of individual human existence and, as we have learned in the proem, the course of virtue on earth, also describes the poet's state of mind. Returning to the opening words of the proem

with this awareness, we realize that the cycle of flourishing
and decay inherent in life's patterns, as the cycle will emerge
in the narrative, also captures the experience of writing a
poem—this poem[11]:

> The waies, through which my weary steps I guyde,
> In this delightfull land of Faery,
> Are so exceeding spacious and wyde,
> And sprinckled with such sweet variety,
> Of all that pleasant is to eare or eye,
> That I nigh rauisht with rare thoughts delight,
> My tedious trauell doe forget thereby;
> And when I gin to feele decay of might,
> It strength to me supplies, and chears my dulled spright.
>
> [Proem, 1]

The poet's own enterprise balances elation and despair at the
same time that it reflects the larger view of life as an involvement in an alternating cycle of growth and decay. His com-
pensation for an apparently inévitable "decay of might" lies
in the renewing pleasance of the journey's "variety." At this
point, then, it is best to remember what Coleridge says of the
ideal poem: "The reader should be carried forward, not
merely or chiefly by the mechanical impulse of curiosity, or
by a restless desire to arrive at the final solution; but by the
pleasurable activity of mind excited by the attractions of the
journey itself . . . at every step he pauses and half recedes,
and from the retrogressive movement collects the force which
again carries him onward."[12]

What is the force, though, that carries this poet onward?
So far in the proem he has had a good deal to say about the
decline of virtue but very little about its renewal. Whatever
force it is, we know from the opening stanza that it appeals
first to his senses, his eyes and his ear, as well as to an inner
faculty, his "rare thoughts delight." The question is
answered in the last stanzas of the proem, where the poet
counterbalances his lament for fallen courtesy in an evil

world with the strengthening, rejuvenating realization that the source of true courtesy also happens to be his own source of poetic inspiration:

> But where shall I in all Antiquity
> So faire a patterne finde, where may be seene
> The goodly praise of Princely curtesie,
> As in your selfe, O soueraine Lady Queene,
> In whose pure minde, as in a mirrour sheene,
> It showes, and with her brightnesse doth inflame
> The eyes of all, which thereon fixed beene;
> But meriteth indeed an higher name:
> Yet so from low to high vplifted is your name.
>
> [Proem, 6]

The neoplatonic cast of the description of the queen seems by virtue of its very exaltedness to renew the poet's confidence in his mission. By deriving virtue from his queen and then returning it to her as an offering, he himself creates an act of courtesy. His personal commitment to courtesy suddenly takes the form of writing a poem about courtesy. The intricate cyclical process that is implied leads him back to the source of virtue itself, embodied in his sovereign.[13]

The role of Gloriana in *The Faerie Queene* poses problems for a modern audience which finds it difficult to understand the adulation so consistently directed toward her in the several proems and introductions. Book 6, however, makes her role more comprehensible, because, even more than earlier, her role is intimate to this book's heart. Not only is she the embodiment of courtesy, as she was the embodiment of chastity in book 3, for example; but also Gloriana is the closest thing the poet knows to virtue itself. This distinction is important in the book that is going to attempt to delineate the differences between courtesy and the essence of virtue. The distinctions will not be clear until Acidale, where the vision will define for the poet the source of both courtesy and virtue.

Much that I have suggested up to this point has perhaps

conveyed the impression that I am in fact arguing for the poet and not Calidore as the hero of book 6. That is not my intention. I do maintain, however, that the unusual identification that critics have increasingly recognized between Calidore and the poet springs not from a confusion about his hero on Spenser's part, but from an impulse to capture life as an integrated, interrelated process. Writing about courtesy means writing about poetry, or as Humphrey Tonkin aptly puts it, "Book VI is a poem talking about itself."[14] Spenser's insistence on two mutually illuminating legends and two heroes is the result of an integrating sensibility that naturally sees life as a whole.

A closer look at Spenser's definition of courtesy justifies reading book 6 as a legend with two blossoms. At the beginning of canto 2 in one of those instructive introductions, the poet suggests that courtesy constitutes the outward manifestation of an inner "good" inherent in all men:

> What vertue is so fitting for a knight,
> Or for a Ladie, whom a knight should loue,
> As Curtesie, to bear themselves aright
> To all of each degree, as doth behoue?
> For whether they be placed high aboue,
> Or low beneath, yet ought they well to know
> Their good, that none them rightly may reproue
> Of rudenesse, for not yeelding what they owe:
> Great skill it is such duties timely to bestow.
>
> Thereto greate helpe dame Nature selfe doth lend:
> For some so goodly gratious are by kind,
> That euery action doth them much commend,
> And in the eyes of men great liking find;
> Which others, that haue greater skill in mind,
> Though they enforce themselues, cannot attaine.
> For euerie thing, to which one is inclin'd,
> Dost best become, and greatest grace doth gaine:
> Yet praise likewise deserue good thewes, enforst with
>     paine.

[2.1,2]

The poet offers a view of human nature that is essentially on two levels: there is a deep inner source of "good" to which everyone, whether he be high above or low beneath, "is inclin'd." Whatever makes people different from one another is not to be found on this inner level, for virtue is a simple birthright of humanity. As in the proem, the poet again claims that virtue has been planted seedlike and mysteriously within man's soul. The cultivation of that buried seed constitutes every man's duty as a civilized creature.

The human capacity for courtesy is never questioned by the poet, although he recognizes the difficulty of its attainment. As the process of making inherent virtue functional and visible, the operation of courtesy is understood as the outward and recognizable signature of the deeper spirit that binds men together. Courtesy is a social phenomenon by which every man recognizes his spiritual, private brotherhood with his fellows.[15] As such, courtesy demands a perfect coordination of inner spirit and outer behavior, a coordination that presupposes the individual's recognition of his own inherent virtue.

Some men, the poet maintains, achieve this coordination effortlessly and naturally, with the result that they "goodly gratious are by kind." Most men, of course, must learn courtesy, and to do so requires stringent discipline: "Great skill it is such duties timely to bestow." Even then, there are others who, though blessed with virtue, cannot acquire courtesy. The poet's task, at least in part, is to praise "good thewes, enforst with paine," to credit the discipline that accompanies the cultivation of natural virtue.

At several stages of the narrative, the poet pauses to reiterate that to be courteous means to "displaye" in outer, literally superficial actions a true inner grace:

> The gentle minde by gentle deedes is knowne.
> For a man by nothing is so well bewrayd,
> As by his manners, in which plaine is showne

Of what degree and what race he is growne.

[3.1]

Or conversely,

> Like as the gentle hart it selfe bewrayes,
> In doing gentle deedes with franke delight,
> Euen so the baser mind it selfe displayes
> In cancred malice and reuengefull spight.

[7.1]

In passages such as these throughout the book a significant pattern works to affect our understanding of human behavior. A spatial composition, one of many employed quietly to do the work of the imagination, places virtue (and baseness) behind or within the outer "deedes" and manners of human intercourse. The poet's vision, it will be remembered, as well as the genesis of virtue itself, partakes of a similar metaphoric composition: a movement from deep within a primal source emanates to the surface of human life. This design signifies a great deal more than the facility of an accomplished poet. The execution of the pattern in the narrative serves vividly as an example of Spenser's ability to coordinate image and theme. It is worth pausing over Calidore's encounter with Tristram as a demonstration of how Spenser accomplishes this delicate coordination.

Chancing to come upon Tristram in combat, Calidore delays approaching and, instead, watches the young man from a distance. Hesitation and observation convince Calidore of Tristram's worth, and he concludes before approaching close enough to speak that the youth is "borne of noble race" (2.5). As a result of their ensuing conversation, Calidore reiterates his original intuition of Tristram's genesis: surely he is "borne of some Heroicke sead," says Calidore. The integration of inner virtue with outer manner is so satisfyingly complete in Tristram that Calidore is forced to recognize a nobility that "in his face appears and gratious godly-head" (2.25).

The episode with Tristram demonstrates another noteworthy manipulation of images that are summoned to underscore the poem's meaning and that are thickly intertangled with other image patterns in the book. Even more persistent than, and indeed closely akin to, the flower image is the repetition of images that suggest sight. A correspondence between "sight" and the deeper faculties of human understanding, variously located in the "mind" and the "heart," is consistent with the spatial composition of other images in the book. Although Spenser lards the narrative with this dual image (sight/mind), his skill conceals the labor of forming the action by means of the image. And so while there is scarcely an incident in the entire book that does not depict someone looking, someone perceiving by means of his visual organ, it is perhaps best to confine attention to the relatively simple locus of canto 2.

The argument proclaims that "Calidore sees young Tristram slay/A proud discourteous knight" and at least twenty-four times in the episode someone is depicted in the act of seeing.[16] Usually, of course, it is Calidore, who uses his visual perception as a means of obtaining facts and verifying the merits of a situation. Fresh from his success with Briana and Crudor, Calidore is said to have "spyde" Tristram "fighting on foot, as well he him descryde." Next to Tristram "a Ladie faire he saw." Before Calidore can respond to his perception in any active way, Tristram slays his foe, an event which, when Calidore 'saw, his hart was inly child." Neverthelesss, Calidore refrains from action, preferring instead a visual scrutiny of the young man's clothing and demeanor: "Him steadfastly he markt and saw to bee/A goodly youth of amiable grace." After "well hauing vewed" this spectacle, Calidore at last follows up his visual examination with a verbal one. Although Tristram's account of the rescue satisfies Calidore's curiosity, it is the ocular proof that arouses the knight's wonder: "but more admyr'd [Calidore] the stroke" of Tristram's spear. "Seeing his face so louely sterne and coy," Calidore can only conclude that this youth must be sprung of some "Heroicke sead" and worthy of trust and squirehood.

Why is Calidore's visual perception such a strong preoccupation? As a means of learning truth and understanding the nature of things, it is important to see and to see clearly. Calidore must rely on visual phenomena as guides to action in a way analogous to the poet's reliance on "all that pleasant is to eare or eye." The senses are the indispensable gateways to the heart (the poet's own "rare thoughts delight"), the physical media that approach truth.

Often, however, mere sight by itself cannot adequately comprehend all of life's profoundest experiences. In the Tristram episode Calidore is able to trust what he sees as a guide to action. By the time he reaches Acidale it is apparent that he needs an understanding that penetrates beyond the visual beauty of the naked maidens. It is not without significance, then, and perhaps goes some way toward explaining Calidore's incomprehension of the vision, that he partakes of the experience solely as visual phenomenon. He is described as

> Beholding all, yet of them vnespyde.
> There he did see, that pleased much his sight,
> That euen he him selfe his eyes enuyde,
> An hundred naked maidens lilly white,
> All raunged in a ring, and dauncing in delight.
>
> [10.11]

Calidore's envy of his own eyes implies a dissociation from himself that can only be ominous in the light of his incomprehension:

> Much wondred *Calidore* at this straunge sight,
> Whose like before his eye had neuer seene,

> And standing long astonished in spright,
> And rapt with pleasaunce, wist not what to weene.
>                                              [10.17]

Calidore's inability to "weene" the meaning of the Vision, to understand what he sees in more than a superficial way, is the most forceful instance in the book of something the poet has underscored from his opening words, something that is summed up in one of this book's most memorable couplets:

> But vertues seat is deepe within the mynd,
> And not in outward shows, but inward thoughts defynd.
>                                              [Proem, 5]

The outward shows even of Acidale, as ravishing as they may be, can induce no more than astonishment, when the viewer sees only with his eye. For inward illumination Calidore must rely on an internal faculty, an insight, capable of fathoming the ravishing outer beauties of the dancing figures and grasping their true hidden meaning.

Returning to the proem with these considerations in the foreground, we immediately find that once again we are meant to understand what follows by the patterns that the proem presents. The poet presents what seem to be two contradictory notions of courtesy as it exists in the contemporary world. His first and negative proposition is that courtesy is a "forgerie" of what it was in plain antiquity,

> Fashion'd to please the eies of them, that pas,
> Which see not perfect things but in a glas:
> Yet is that glasse so gay, that it can blynd
> The wisest sight, to think gold that is bras.
>                                              [Proem, 5]

The superficiality of the poet's contemporaries, depicted by their exclusive and shallow use of their "eies," leads only to blindness. In the next stanza, however, the poet qualifies his originally total disparagement of the present age, when he turns to the queen's court. The mirror that deceived his contemporaries in one stanza reflects a pure mind in the next:

> But where shall I in all Antiquity
> So faire a patterne finde, where may be seene
> The goodly praise of Princely curtesie,
> As in your selfe, O soueraine Lady Queene,
> In whose pure minde, as in a mirrour sheene,
> It showes, and with her brightnesse doth inflame
> The eyes of all, which thereon fixed beene.
>
> [Proem, 6]

The poet's two opposing uses of the "glas" to describe an act of perception both derive from long traditions, of course; but whether the glass is a speculum of truth or something through which we see darkly, the poet's indecision about the state of courtesy in his world seems no more well defined. The paradox is clarified only if we move back a few stanzas to the poet's discussion of his vocation. "Reuele to me the sacred noursery/Of virtue," he asks the Muses, where it "does hidden ly/From view of men, and wicked worlds disdaine." The process of bringing virtue into open view defines the poet's conception of his poetry. His narrative is the means of making visible what would otherwise remain hidden from his contemporaries' sight. In this endeavor he is abetted by the queen herself, who in her very person ("your selfe") makes virtue visible.

 This is exactly what courtesy does; it makes virtue a reality in the day-to-day life and relations of men. The proper exercise of courtesy requires that one *see* in both senses of the word: one must see and perceive accurately (as Calidore does in the opening cantos), and one must also envision the secret source of virtue that his courtesy will quicken into action. Just as the queen's courtiers must have the outer brightness of her inner virtue on which to concentrate, so Calidore must coordinate his outer "manners mild" with his inner "gentlenesse of spright."

As often as "sight" is the perceptual agency in book 6, then, it is matched by repetition of words such as "mind," and "spright," and "heart." The centers of truth are portrayed spatially as within ("vertues seat is deep within the mynd"), just as the initial, albeit often limited, approach to truth is suggested by the physical, external act of seeing. Because virtue's garden lies hidden from sight, and accessible only to "the mindes of mortall men," Calidore and the poet each must find within himself the seeds of virtue before he can actualize the truths that reside there.

In the narrative the several strands that I have been unraveling are woven with such virtuosity that the main impression is one of effortlessness. As a result of an intimate verbal resonance there exists an almost secret poetic harmony among the disparate episodes of the adventure. The "ensample" of Mirabella, for one, is rendered more significant by the interplay of earlier motifs. Details such as the "proud looks" and "goodly hew" that allow her "with the onely twinckle of her eye" to "kindle louely fire/In th' harts of many a knight" (7. 28-31) summon up other uses of those images to assist our inspection and subsequent evaluation of Mirabella's behavior. As often happens in the middle or "forest" cantos, the poet charges the particulars of his language, rather than the continuity of character or action, with the task of integrating the narrative with the spirit of the overall design.

The relatively uncomplicated episode of Crudor and Briana exemplifies the general pattern while offering some interesting variations. Having left Artegall in pursuit of the beast, Calidore encounters a comely squire who has been "bound" to a tree by Crudor's Seneschall. In fact, the episode is filled with images of binding and constriction, and as usual a double purpose is served. Courtesy as practiced by Calidore must first break the oppressive bonds of inhumane discourtesy in an action that suggests the liberation of hidden virtue from the chains of fallen life. On the other hand, the courteous man must learn a new form of constriction: the paradoxically happy discipline of the "bands of ciuilitie" that unite all men. Crudor has bound Briana to the discourteous task of lining his mantle with the beards of knights and locks of ladies. Castle Maleffort itself malevolently encircles those within, and, when he tries to enter, Calidore is "flockt" about by its guardsmen. The description of his combat is revealing:

> Like as a water streame, whose swelling sourse
> Shall driue a Mill, within strong bancks is pent,
> And long restrayned of his ready course;
> So soone as passage is vnto him lent,
> Breakes forth, and makes his way more violent
> Such was the fury of Sir *Calidore*.
>
> [1.21]

The release of the restrained stream breaking forth graphically illustrates the power of courtesy in action.

Where we would expect a similar sense of liberation to ensue once Calidore takes on his remaining adversaries, we instead find him employing devices that resemble their own discourteous restriction. He confines Briana to her castle and in battle pins Crudor to the ground, thanks, let it be noted, to Calidore's "quick[ness] of sight." All this provides the knight with the opportunity to pronounce to his captive that

> In vaine he seeketh others to suppresse,
> Who hath not learnd him selfe first to subdew.
>
> [1.31]

Because Crudor has not yet learned that courtesy is a self-subduing discipline that brings with it a new freedom, Calidore must teach him by force.

"Seeing, in what danger" Crudor is placed and beholding his conversion from her castle wall, Briana comes forth

All ouercome with infinite affect,
For [Calidore's] exceeding courtesie, that pearst
Her stubborne hart with inward deepe effect
Before his feet her self did proiect.

[1.45]


A visual spectacle has penetrated her heart, the seat of virtue which is the due of her common humanity, and thereby prompts her conversion to the liberating bonds of civility.

It is in the light of these various considerations that we may best approach the pastoral cantos where the two journeys of poet and hero, which divide the book uneasily between them, are finally brought together. Spenser's pursuit of images such as "mind" and "heart" suggests that withdrawal and inner transformation will provide the means for the moral regeneration of poet and hero alike. The resonance of these and other images prepares for the introduction of a pastoral retreat at the climax of the book. The pastoral world is the embodiment, the environmental re-creation of the somewhat nebulous and discreet suggestions that the book's recurring images have encouraged. The images that seem to have been scattered randomly through the narrative have in fact been carefully sown and are ready to flourish, as the poet's self-depiction as a ploughman at the beginning of the pastoral cantos intimates.

Behind all pastoral works lie certain literary assumptions which Renaissance poets exploit, and which, of course, Spenser himself helped to make acceptable. One assumption provides that pastoral be taken by the reader as an extended figure of withdrawal and of a return to human origins. This is an obvious point, but it needs stressing. As Calidore retreats from the court and city "back" (9.3) to the farms and finally to the fields and flocks of the pastoral world, a dramatic sense of "return," a sense that the narrator has previously provided in his nostalgia for "plaine Antiquitie," forces itself into consideration.[17] The sacred nursery of virtue, the unploughed soil of the poet's art, the flower-decked cottage of the hermit all presage and contribute to the meaning of the pastoral cantos. Spenser relies, here and elsewhere, on the more or less automatic responses that the introduction of a time-worn literary convention would induce in his audience. The freedom that this expectation gives to the poet cannot be underestimated in coming to terms with this book. Rather than exploit those responses for either satirical or sentimental purposes, however, Spenser sustains interest in the problem of defining courtesy by placing his hero in a literary environment familiar to his audience.

The pastoral environment fulfills the prerequisities for finding courtesy. As the outward and visible sign of the virtue inherent in all men, courtesy demands the individual's awareness of his own virtue. The courteous man must see that the seeds of virtue have been planted in the hidden nursery of his soul, and he must cultivate those seeds to burst forth to honor. In one form or another, courtesy actually necessitates a return to the primal state of innocence and virtue. As a practical discipline it first requires the individual's recognition that beneath the dross of his fallen condition lies a remnant of his original perfection. Calidore's return to the pastoral world, where both courtesy and its source, virtue, exist in ways that they do not in the court, answers the poet's nostalgia for the golden days of antiquity. At the same time, Calidore's return, as every reader of pastoral knows, reenacts the journey of the individual back to his own hidden genetic nursery. In this sense, pastoral (or some version of pastoral) is required by the legend of courtesy. Pastoral provides the setting that is necessary if the hero is to find courtesy, to return to human origins in a place that has never known the forgeries and falseness of civilized life. Such a return has also been the poet's wish for himself, a wish he makes explicit when he asks the Muses to reveal to him the sacred nursery of virtue, hidden like the pastoral world itself "from view of men, and wicked worlds disdaine." The poet's resumption of

Calidore's quest at the crucial point when the knight enters the pastoral world underscores how both of them together have returned to the green nursery of virtue.

The frailty of that world and the continuously ambiguous situations and problematic characters that it contains perhaps reflect the uncertainty and ambivalence present in the mind of the poem's creator. Any attempt to return to a world unhampered by the evils of society is as futile, and at the same time as compelling, as the poet's attempt to cultivate an imperishable flower from the nursery of virtue. The human spirit yearning for a lost perfection is perhaps capable of achieving it, but only momentarily. Calidore's challenge, as well as the poet's, is to embody that fleeting vision in the world of action, to make it, one could say, useful.

The pastoral cantos, then, depict the slow, often painful, but nonetheless persistent disciplinary process that eventually leads Calidore to Acidale and to Colin Clout's tutelage. His transformation is not sudden. He enters the pastoral world as a representative of the court. His stay there teaches him to strip away the courtly trappings that are part of his inheritance as an exemplar of a debased courtesy. The differences between the courtly world in which Calidore shines as one of the most sterling figures and the simpler, happier world in which he retreats is a measure of how far courtesy is from what it was. The Blattant Beast is unknown to the denizens of a world of seclusion and withdrawal. Maliboe recounts his youthful sojourn to tend the courtly gardens in order to demonstrate the contrast between the dazzling forgeries of those gardens and the life-enhancing beauty of the pastoral *hortus*. His "return" to his "natiue home" (9.25) carries an ontological dimension, as does his rescue of the foundling Pastorella:

> [He f]ound her by fortune, which to him befell,
> In th' open fields an Infant left alone,
> And taking vp brought home.
>
> [9.14]

Whatever Calidore's motives in wanting to remain, it is at least certain that the beauty of Pastorella expresses the beauty and security of her environment. His first view finds her, flower-like, enclosed in concentric circles of companions,

> . . . round about
> Enuiron'd with a girland, goodly graced,
> Of louely lasses, and them all without
> The lustie shepheard swaynes sate in a rout.
>
> [9.8]

Many features of the pastoral world echo the poet's other attempts to render the sources of virtue. Like the queen surrounded by her courtiers, or like the vision of the Graces itself, Pastorella is literally contained by her admirers. "Being bred vnder base shepheards wings" (9.35), she becomes a living emblem of the secret sources that both make courtesy possible and inspire the poet. It is not surprising, then, to find the word "mind" as well as other images of inner understanding attached to Pastorella frequently; "though meane her lot, yet higher did her mind ascend"; "in her brest" she found no place for Coridon. Calidore's attempt to win her love means, in short, that he must somehow aproach her hidden nursery. He must make himself worthy by an appeal to the inner center of virtue which she in fact embodies.

This is no mean feat, for it requires Calidorc to embrace a new understanding of human relations. The courtly glitter of the gold that offends Meliboe has no place in the pastoral renewal of values. And so, Calidore's dangerous preoccupation with outward appearance, whereby Pastorella becomes the "obiet of his vew/On which his hungry eye was always bent" (9.26), must be adjusted.[18] For her part, Pastorella will have none of his "courteous guize"; "his layes, his loues, his looks she did them all despize" (9.35). Characteristically enough so early in his pastoral education, Calidore is prompted by her scorn "to chaunge the manner of his loftie looke" (9.36) by outfitting himself in lowly shepherd's garb. This is the beginning, the outer manifestation of his change.

If Calidore's transformation were merely sartorial, of course, there would be little to commend him as the knight of courtesy. As the poet has both stated and dramatized, outward show and adornment must coincide with the essence of the courteous mind. Calidore's change of clothing, as the first step in his discovery of virtue, is accompanied by a similar demonstration of courtesy in action. He gladly undertakes the chores of pastoral life and commends himself in sport and dance. His prowess in a wrestling match shines all the more admirably when accompanied by his generosity to his opponent, the childish Corydon.

Although in canto 9 Calidore goes a long way as the courteous knight toward making virtue plain, it is not until after the vision, or more properly, until after Colin Clout has elucidated the vision for him, that Calidore seems to attain the understanding necessary to continue his quest. I say "seems" because no such understanding is explicit. As many have noted, there is no statement of Calidore's enlightenment as a result of the vision. Nevertheless, it cannot be without significance that Pastorella's love for him blossoms after the vision and not before. The importance of the vision to their love is affirmed, in the oblique way of this book, in terms of a characteristic metaphor. Before the vision Calidore's courtesy has already

> . . . surely wrought
> With this faire Mayd, and in her mynde the seeds
> Of perfect loue did sow.
> 
> [9.45]

The love he plants in her mind, like the flower on a lowly stalk and the poet's poem, grows quietly until after the vision. Only then, after having rescued Pastorella from the tiger in a significant display of heroic valor, does Calidore enjoy the benefits of his nurture:

So well he wood her . .
That of his loue he reapt the timely frute,
And ioyed long in close felicity.

[10.28]

As the organic metaphor has often suggested in this book, however, their happiness together can be only temporary. The "bitter storme of foule adversity" (10.38) will destroy the lovers' joy along with the whole pastoral world as inevitably as youth yields to age and innocence to bitter experience.

The episode on Mount Acidale that leads Calidore to Pastorella's love encompasses two distinct experiences that exist fleetingly as one. The first is Calidore's vision of the Graces, who embody virtue and teach men how to make virtue visible through courtesy. The second is the poet's vision of Colin piping to his country lass. The Graces and Colin's "fourth Mayd" dance and sing together only while Calidore, hidden away in the woods, watches them. They vanish altogether when he advances toward them. Only in that instant, only as long as Calidore watches enraptured from afar, does the vision exist as a completely unified totality. This is the moment when the poet speaks directly to us his audience, in one of his three significant direct addresses in the Acidale episode:

Looke how the Crowne, which *Ariadne* wore
Vpon her yuory forehead that same day,
That *Theseus* her vnto his bridale bore,
When the bold *Centaures* made that bloudy fray,
With the fierce *Lapithes*, which did them dismay;
Being now placed in the firmament,
Through the bright heauen doth her beams display,
And is vnto the starres an ornament,
Which rownd about her moue in order excellent.

[10.23]

Most readers have sensed the importance of these strange and confusing lines, with their disturbing mixture of violence and heavenly order.[19] Actually that disturbance captures something of the book viewed as an artistic whole. Ariadne's crown, like the garland on the head of Pastorella, could not protect her from the violence that surrounded her. Her crown was an ornament of an inner beauty that could find no place in the bloody frays of life. As an emblem of order, Ariadne's crown, and, it may be said, the vision that the poet is now describing, acquires its meaning as an ornament of the heavens, distant and mysterious. So also, the "beauty of this goodly band" dancing before Calidore's astonished eyes cannot provide him with a vision of beauty that will radically change the harshness of life.

"Suche was the beauty of this goodly band," the poet continues, as he proceeds to explain their meaning as best he can. His apprehension of the vision, it should be noted, while more complete than Calidore's, is nonetheless imperfect. The poet knows that these are the Graces, who "all gifts of grace do graunt," but his understanding of the scene extends not much more deeply than that observation. In fact, the poet himself is affected by the vision, with Calidore, while he witnesses it. His joy is that of a participant in the vision, not merely that of the retrospective narrator. It is for this reason that the poet too must be instructed by Colin Clout, and the instruction begins when the poet suddenly, rapturously comprehends exactly who the jolly shepherd's lass in the midst of the Graces is (16). His realization that the fourth maid is the source of Colin's inspiration impels him to interrupt the narrative again, this time in a direct address to Colin Clout:

> Pype iolly shepheard, pype thou now apace
> Vnto thy loue, that made thee low to lout:
> Thy loue is present there with thee in place,
> Thy loue is there aduaunst to be another Grace.
> [10.16]

While Calidore continues to gaze on the spectacle uncomprehendingly, the poet has apprehended a bond between

himself and Colin, who is now before us in his quintessential-
ly orphic role. Their affinity as poets will not be firmly
cemented until later in the episode when Colin explains the visions more completely. The poet has nonetheless begun to
realize that he has witnessed an act of poetic inspiration.
Colin's evocation of the Graces, who make courtesy visible,
is nothing other than a performance of the poetic act itself.
The effects of Colin's piping are as ravishing as they are
mysterious, and the poet's unusual intrusion to address Colin
marks his own ardent discovery of this truth.

Calidore's interruption dispels this remarkably brief vision.
The episode as a whole, however, is not at all complete. Both
Calidore and the poet have in succession witnessed something
intimately related to their respective quests. It now remains
for Colin Clout to explain that vision, and to deepen its
viewers' understanding of it; he does so not only for Calidore
but also for the poet. Colin has evoked the Graces, that is, he
has made them visible, just as Calidore must learn to make
virtue visible, and just as the poet hopes to make his virtuous
story visible. And so Colin directs his discourse first to
Calidore, then to the poet, in a repetition of the sequence in
which the vision has just been experienced.

Colin's instruction to Calidore embellishes and deepens
the poet's earlier assertion that the Graces bestow their gifts
on all men. Now Colin explains that their nakedness is the
natural reflection of guilelessness and inner virtue. They
stand "simple and true from couert malice free," an embodiment of the courteous integration of outer beauty and inner
virtue.

> These three on men all gracious gifts bestow,
> Which decke the body or adorne the mynde,
> To make them louely or well fauoured show,
> As comely carriage, entertainment kynde,
> Sweete semblaunt, friendly offices that bynde,
> And all the complements of curtesie.
>
> [10.23]

We might well have questioned the importance of the courtesy that Colin defines if all that has preceded had not served to color and shape the meaning of his description. The "well fauoured show" that the Graces bestow, if understood apart from the rest of the book, would seem to be only the superficial trappings of courtly intercourse. The efforts of the poet up until the vision, however, have made such a misunderstanding impossible, because the outward sign of true courtesy is the expression of an inward beauty.

Having explained the Graces to Calidore, Colin attempts to explain the meaning of the country lass in the Graces' midst. This chore he finds difficult, because he is not even sure who she is:

> Who can aread what creature mote she bee,
> Whether a creature, or a goddesse graced
> With heauenly gifts from heuen first enraced?
>
> [10.25]

Colin's uncertainty is the reader's as well. More mysterious than even the Graces, the fourth maid seems to be divine in origin. The refulgent light with which Colin surrounds her in his description—

> So farre as doth the daughter of the day,
> All other lesser lights in light excell,—
>
> [10.26]

has been paralleled in this book only by Gloriana herself, and indeed this similarity does not escape the poet. Here, within the circle of the Graces, stands a maid so divine that she seems to outshine the Graces themselves:

> Diuine resemblaunce, beauty soueraine rare;
> Firme Chastity, that spite ne blemish dare;
> All which she with such courtesie doth grace,
> That all her peres cannot with her compare,

But quite are dimmed, when she is in place.
She made me often pipe and now to pipe apace.
[10.27]

Colin's maid, in fact, seems remarkably to be the embodiment of virtue itself. Her "beauty soueraine rare," neoplatonically exalted, suggests the country lass as the source of virtue, the unapproachable center made visible in the actions of courtesy.[20] She bears to the Graces who encircle and emanate from her a relationship that virtue, hidden within the secret nursery of the human spirit, bears to the manners mild of civilized behavior.

With Colin's simple concluding statement that "she often made me pipe and now to pipe apace" comes again the realization for the poet that this maid is also the source of poetic inspiration. He interrupts the narrative for the third and last time as his mission is suddenly renewed:

Sunne of the world, great glory of the sky,
That all the earth doest lighten with thy rayes,
Great *Gloriana*, greatest Maiesty,
Pardon thy shepheard, mongst so many layes,
As he hath sung of thee in all his dayes,
To make one minime of thy poor handmayd,
And underneath thy feete to place her prayse,
That when thy glory shall be farre displayed
To future age of her this mention may be made.
[10.28]

Guiding his weary steps through the book's labyrinths, the poet has not mentioned Gloriana since the proem. Now suddenly he has been provided with a "patterne" of his own role as a poet by the example of Colin piping to his country lass. For one instant, perhaps the only necessary instant, his mission becomes comprehensible, and the future of his poem stands firm. With the clarity of *Colin Clouts Come Home Againe* the poet envisions his poem and indeed his whole career as a monument to the virtue that his queen embodies.

The future does not close to darkness; the poem itself, the whole epic of his career, will enlighten future ages with its display of virtue.

The final stanzas of the book qualify but do not destroy the poet's joy at the time of the vision. The pessimism of the conclusion, which finds the beast at large in the world and the poet's "homely verse" prey to the wicked tongues of backbiters, ought to be accepted in the same unsettling spirit that the vision of Acidale concludes. Readers have found the vision, like the conclusion, distressing for good reasons. Surely it ought to "mean" something. How can a glimpse of so divine a spectacle not affect Calidore more deeply? The fact is, though, that the vision has as little direct effect as Ariadne's crown, fixed in the firmament, has for mortals here below who admire its beauty. The vision is as uncertainly relevant to life, as briefly sustained, as the pastoral world harboring the vision is to the courtly world. Like poetry, visions never seem to change things; or if they do, we cannot know how or why. Perhaps Calidore wins Pastorella as a result of what he saw on Acidale. Spenser suggests this as a possibility, but only a possibility. Perhaps Calidore eventually subdues the beast precisely *because* he learned something about courtesy in the pastoral world or *because* he was privileged to see the Graces. These claims are never literally maintained; there is no explicit causal connection between Calidore's success, which by any standard can only be seen as partial, and the truths he glimpses on Acidale. No tidy formula is advanced about the necessity of the vision to the fulfillment of the quest. To have suggested one would have been a violation of the spirit in which this book is conceived.

What happens after the vision in the rest of the book fulfills, however, the cyclic process of flourishing and decay that does constitute the spirit of this book. "Fortune," that omnipresent force that disrupts where it lists, follows Calidore even into Arcadia. Inescapable mutability brings the destructive Brigants as surely as the seasons rotate. Calidore's failure to subdue the beast is repeated, the poet tells us, by one after another of "his brethren borne in Britaine land" (12.39), and their failures have left us in a dark and noisome world.

Yet as unremitting as death and chaos are, the strength of man to renew himself, to be born again like Pastorella, is equally insistent. The deadly shade of the Brigant's cave that nearly destroys her cannot extinguish the flower of her beauty, which "like a rose her silken leaues did faire vnfold" (12.7). Pastorella's journey from the cradle of the green world to the infernal darkness of the underground cave and finally to restoration in her parents' arms enacts the cycle of human existence that we find everywhere in book 6. The pastoral world, the youth of Calidore, and the poet's work share a fragile, evanescent beauty that is as vulnerable as human decay and mortality are inescapable. Buried deep within every man lies the hidden nursery of virtue planted in the remote past of the race. The very attempt to discover it, the awkward process of making virtue a part of fallen experience is the aim of the courteous man and the mission of the responsible poet.

# Conclusion

*In* their differing and often oblique ways the pastorals of Spenser and Milton recreate idylls of the elevated imagination. They thoroughly exploit the features of pastoral that make it a unique literary mode: its multidimensional distance from the common world of social experience, from the mimetic art that often reflects that experience, and even from the natural world in which pastoral pretends to be located. Each of their pastorals exults in its own autonomy. Growing into another nature, the poet can rest serenely in the golden light of the environment which constitutes living proof of his erected wit. But what value do such poems have for anyone but the poet? This question must always be raised when we read the work of poets whose expressed intention is to make their gifts accessible and useful to their readers. The imaginations of Spenser and Milton can never rest easy if cut off from the mundane world each poet believes to be in need of his art for its betterment. This is the dilemma that Spenser's and Milton's pastorals recurrently pose: the self-reliance of the poet's inner world, midway between Arcadia and the fallen world, contradicts the poet's conviction that he possesses an indispensable vision, which is his duty to impart, about how life ought to be lived. Each poet's resolution of this contradition underscores essential differences between their entire imaginative orientations.

The contradiction itself reflects the quandary behind all Renaissance animadversions about the value of literature. The theorists of the day confront a dilemma similar to that of Spenser's and Milton's pastorals when they attempt to square literature as a delightful activity with its more serious function as an enterprise of moral elucidation. Their solutions, though by no means simple, fairly consistently hinge on belief in the poet as a light-bringer to men. Sidney's argument, to choose a familiar exemplar, goes like this: the poet's invention produces something beyond nature, and furthermore, something *better* than the nature we live in. The ideal world of the poet for Sidney and others exists in such a way that the reader is moved to emulate it in his own life. In its fullness and concreteness, poetry and its heroes teach the reader to avoid vice and pursue virtue. "If the Poet doe his part a-right, he will shew you in *Tantalus, Atreus* and such like, nothing that is not to be shunned; in *Cyrus, Aeneas, Vlisses,* each thing to be followed."[1] Finding the world of poetry too delightful to be resisted, the reader is moved to emulate the examples so passionately set before him.

The role of the reader, then, in the Renaissance concept of poetry is absolutely crucial. While Sidney devotes much energy to describing the poem and the poet, as both maker and *vates,* his final analysis of what goes into the total design of literature places the reader centrally in view. In order to do his job properly, the poet must be aware of his audience: whom is he addressing, what do his readers have in common, how ought he to present his poem for maximum effect?

One path followed by legions of pastoral poets leads in the direction of satire and allegory. Sanctioned by the examples of Petrarch and Mantuan, the eclogue that glances at greater matters from beneath the pastoral veil provides the poet with a convenient means of endowing his work with social value. Spenser finds this method attractive enough not only for the "moral" eclogues of the *Calender* but also, in a very different way, for *Colin Clouts Come Home Againe.* By subjecting the conventions of pastoral to the requirements of allegory and satire, the poet thrusts his eclogues into the day-to-day world of his reader. He thereby justifies his endeavor by bestowing upon it social and political significance. While most modern readers find this strain of pastoral literature unrewarding, nobody can deny its popularity and longevity.

For the most part, though, allegorical satire is not the path chosen by Spenser and Milton. Their method runs directly contrary. Rather than constructing poems that intrude upon the reader's mundane experience, Spenser and Milton draw the reader into the world of the poem. The reader's engage-ment, under conditions discussed in previous pages, frees him from the limitations of his personal history as he enters a sphere alien to his daily experience. He may then be guided according to the poet's stratagem. The poet may lead us even-tually to Acidale, or he may finally enunciate the genesis of love. He may gradually arrive at a vision of Lycidas or Dido in the joys of heavenly bliss or look forward to a time when all heaven will be shown before our eyes. He may even show us how *not* to conduct our lives: we must beware the pitfalls of Colin's hopeless passion for Rosalind, just as we must learn to transcend the pleasure of L'Allegro in favor of the joy of Il Penseroso. But the achievement of the visionary mo-ment is the distinguishing goal of their pastoral poems, the point they lead us to, as we follow the trail of their heroes through the pastoral landscape.

The divergent attitudes toward the landscape in Spenser's and Milton's pastoral epitomize their differences regarding their vocation. Spenser reposes a greater trust than Milton does in the independent power of the imagination to call up visions. Colin Clout, however momentary or even at times in-effective his powers, achieves his most splendid moments without divine aid. For Milton the unaided imagination can be only an imperfect instrument in the recovery of bliss. Like the landscape it bodies forth, the poetic faculty is inextricable from fallen life and must therefore submit to the strain of a higher mood. A comparison of Colin's performance in "April" to that of the Genius of the Wood in *Arcades* comprises a compact envoy of the two poets' pastorals.

While *Arcades*'s occasion as a courtly entertainment does not of course typify its author's canon, in the figure of the Genius Milton invests many of the qualities he reserves elsewhere for his divinely sanctioned poet-speakers. Like the poet of the "Nativity" ode, the Genius stands midway between the "low world" of "mortal sense" and the "celestial *Sirens* harmony" of the upper regions. Without his attendance the landscape would fall prey to all the corruption that burdens mortal life:

> And all my Plants I save from nightly ill,
> Of noisom winds, and blasting vapors chill.
> And from the Boughs brush off the evil dew,
> And heal the harms of thwarting thunder blew.
>
> [48-51]

None of these features that characterize the Genius would sit well on Colin Clout as we see him in "Aprill." The typically Miltonic use of the first person to vaunt the speaker's powers collides with Colin's preference for actually demonstrating what he can achieve in the celebration of Eliza. The Genius, furthermore, makes far more than Colin would of his unique intermediary position between the natural and celestial realms.

But the most telling difference between the two characters is to be found where they seem most alike. Colin instructs and organizes the rural participants in the celebration of Eliza in much the same way that the Genius orchestrates the nymphs and shepherds of the masque in their obeisance to the "Goddess bright." "Helpe me to blaze/Her worthy praise," says Colin to the nymphs of the countryside, an injunction echoed by the Genius when he informs his Arcadian audience that the divine harmony to which he has access is "worthiest . . . to blaze/The peerless height of her immortal praise" (74-75).

But here the resemblance ends. For Colin spiritual beauty inheres in the landscape. Eliza appears perfectly at home in the pastoral environment and needs only the enhancement of his poetic adornment to rise up in the shepherds' midst. The Genius, however, far from finding his rural queen in the low world of "mortal sense," must lead his followers away from the wood he sanctifies to another locale. His skill, we may say, works almost in spite of the physical landscape he ministers to; he employs nature as a starting point from which to work in the direction of a vision "whose luster leads [him] on" (76). As he approches the goddess bright, the Genius leaves behind the pastoral landscape he has presided over.

In his three very different incarnations, Colin Clout surpasses nature by means of nature. His celebration of Eliza in "Aprill" takes its music from the landscape, is "tuned . . . vnto the Waters fall" (36). In the course of the hymn itself Colin decks Eliza in the ornaments he finds scattered around him in nature's profusion. He has no need to summon an extraterrestrial agent in creating his vision, because his unique gifts bring forth the wondrous from nature's bounty. He accomplishes the *furor poeticus* of his vision of Love in *Colin Clout* in a similar way. He gradually transcends the green world not by rejecting it, but by totally embracing (or re-embracing) its beauty. His greatest, most purely mystical vision is achieved in the heart of pastoral tranquility on Mount Acidale, where he brings forth from the landscape "diuine resemblaunce, beauty soueraine rare" (10.27).

Milton's treatment of the landscape confirms that he does not share Spenser's confidence in the poet's ability to attain exalted spiritual awareness within and through nature. Indeed, as the otherworldly heralds of *Lycidas* suggest, such awareness must often be delivered from a supernatural realm. Unlike Colin Clout, who arrives at his most triumphant visions in the midst of nature by embracing and exploiting her riches, Milton's poets achieve their noblest statements by

ultimately rejecting the natural world in favor of the heavenly
that nature can only mime. A sensitivity to the flaws and inherent corruption of natural life inhibits Milton's poetic
spokesmen from attaining the heightened state that Colin is
capable of in the green world. The landscape in Milton's
poems is presented as a tarnished image of lost perfection,
which as part of fallen life in general must be adjusted and
subordinated to a higher vision of the heavenly environment.
Whereas for Spenser the beauty of the landscape is enhanced
by opening on to a vision almost divine, for Milton supernatural understanding decidedly diminishes the beauty of the
landscape. We must always respond to the sinister side of
man's natural home when we look at Milton's landscapes; the
horrid shrieks and groans of the pagan deities always haunt
the "spring and dale/Edg'd with poplar pale" ("Nativity"
ode, 184-85). Those poems in which Milton employs a significant amount of natural detail—even, finally, *Paradise
Lost*—leave the reader with a far different feeling about the
landscape than do Spender's pastorals. Having gained sight
of a paradise within, happier far than the landscape of the
poem, the reader joins the poet in turning his back on the
garden. Although the legend of courtesy reminds us that in
Spenser Eden may be destroyed, its destruction is not
preliminary to the truest joys of the spirit. Nature and super-
nature for Spenser are part of a continuum within the
cosmos; for Milton, the two are often in contest, perhaps irreconcilable.

This radical division of attitudes between the two poets
toward the landscape, toward pastoral poetry, and finally
toward the poetic vocation ought not to obscure what their
pastorals share. In the pastoral poems where Spenser and
Milton allow themselves free play to ponder the art of poetry
we find them making poetry itself a metaphor of moral
capability. Both poets' claims to authority in their pastorals
depend upon the reader's response to the poet's connections
with literary history and to his ability to discern patterns in

the fragments of fallen life. Good poets, their pastoral poems say, enlighten our lives to the extent that we momentarily assume the pastoral poet's detached vision, that we assent to the conviction that "the poet only bringeth his own stuff, and doth not learn a conceit out of a matter, but maketh a matter for a conceit."[2]

# List of Abbreviations

*ELH: English Literary History*
*PMLA: Publications of the Modern Language Association*
*SEL: Studies in English Literature, 1500-1900*
*SP: Studies in Philology*
*TSLL: Texas Studies in Literature and Language*
*UTQ: University of Toronto Quarterly*

# Notes

## Introduction

1. Recently there have been three noteworthy treatments of both poets simultaneously: Patrick Cullen, *The Infernal Triad: The Flesh, The World, and The Devil in Spenser and Milton* (Princeton, Princeton University Press, 1974); Kathleen Williams, "Milton, Greatest Spenserian," in *Milton and the Line of Vision*, ed. Joseph A. Wittreich, Jr. (Madison: University of Wisconsin Press, 1975), pp. 25-55; A. Kent Hieatt, *Chaucer, Spenser, Milton; Mythopoeic Continuities and Transformations* (Montreal: McGill-Queen's University Press, 1975). See also James Holly Hanford, *A Milton Handbook*, 4th ed. (New York: Appleton, 1974), pp. 259-63; Edwin Greenlaw, "A Better Teacher Than Aquinas," *SP* 14 (1917): 196-217; Greenlaw, "Spenser's Influence on *Paradise Lost*," *SP* 17 (1920): 320-59; Thomas Greene, *The Descent from Heaven: A Study in Epic Continuity* (New Haven: Yale University Press, 1963).

2. The preface to the second book of "The Reason of Church Government," *John Milton: Complete Poems and Major Prose,* ed. Merritt Y. Hughes (New York: Odyssey Press, 1957), p. 669. All references to Milton's prose and all translations of his Latin poetry will be from this edition. All references to Milton's poetry will be from *The Works of John Milton,* ed. Frank Allen Patterson et al. (New York: Columbia University Press, 1931-38).

3. From the letter to Raleigh in *The Works of Edmund Spenser: A Variorum Edition*, ed. Edwin Greenlaw et al. (Baltimore: The Johns Hopkins Press, 1932-57), vol. 1, hereafter referred to as *Variorum*. All references to Spenser's works will be from this edition.

4. A. Bartlett Giamatti, *The Earthly Paradise and the Renaissance Epic* (Princeton: Princeton University Press, 1966), pp. 233-355, writes about Spenser's and Milton's epic "pastoral retreats." The classic locus for a comparison of the differences between Eden and Acrasia's bower is C. S. Lewis, *The Allegory of Love: A Study in Medieval Traditon* (Oxford: Oxford University Press, 1936), pp. 324-33.

5. *An Apology for Poetry*, ed. Geoffrey Shepherd (London: Nelson and Sons Ltd., 1965), p. 116. All references to the *Apology* will be from this edition.

6. From E. K.'s dedicatory epistle to *The Shepheardes Calender*, in *Variorum*, vol. 7, pt. 1, p.10.

7. *The Book Named the Governor*, ed. S. E. Lehmberg (New York: Everyman's Library, 1961), p.31.

8. George Puttenham, *The Arte of English Poesie*, ed. Gladys D. Willcock and Alice Walker (Cambridge: Cambridge University Press, 1936), p. 39; *Apology*, p. 116.

9. *The Works of Michael Drayton*, ed. J. William Hebel (Oxford: Basil Blackwell, 1932), 2:517.

10. *John Milton: Complete Poems*, ed. M. Hughes, p. 668.

## Chapter 1

1. "Timber: or, Discoveries," in *Literary Criticism of Seventeenth-Century England*, ed. Edward W. Tayler (New York: Knopf, Inc., 1967), p.135.

2. Samuel Johnson, "Milton," in *Lives of the English Poets,* ed. G. B. Hill (Oxford: Clarendon Press, 1905), 1: 163-165.

3. Cf. Thomas G. Rosenmeyer, *The Green Cabinet: Theocritus and the European Pastoral Lyric* (Berkeley and Los Angeles: University of California Press, 1969), p. 196, who sees no "fatal jarring of the central idea" in Virgil's alteration of the Theocritean setting.

4. A substantial and elegant treatment is provided by Harry Levin, *The Myth of the Golden Age in the Renaissance* (Bloomington and London: University of Indiana Press, 1969).

5. "A Discourse on Pastoral," in *Alexander Pope: Selected Poetry and Prose*, ed. W. K. Wimsatt, Jr. (New York: Holt, Rinehart, 1951), p.9.

6. "Select Translations from Scaliger's *Poetics*," ed. and trans. F. M. Padelford, *Yale Studies in English* 26 (1905): 21.

7. From an untitled poem by "J. M." in *England's Helicon*, ed. Hugh MacDonald (Cambridge, Mass.: Harvard University Press, 1962), pp. 33-34.

8. *Virgil: The Pastoral Poems*, trans. E. B. Rieu (London: Penguin Books, 1949). All references to the *Eclogues* and all translations will be from this volume.

9. I have paraphrased lines 63-65.

10. The best treatment of Virgil's pastoral persona is provided by Eleanor Winsor Leach, *Virgil's "Eclogues": Landscapes of Experience* (Ithaca and London: Cornell University Press, 1974), pp. 345-377.

11. See Bruno Snell, *The Discovery of The Mind: The Greek Origins of European Thought*, trans. T. G. Rosenmeyer (Cambridge, Mass.: Harvard University Press, 1953), pp. 295-299.

12. "The Renaissance Imagination: Second World and Green World," *The Centennial Review* 9 (1965): 36-78.

13. The Oaten Flute: *Essays on Pastoral Poetry and the Pastoral Ideal* (Cambridge, Mass.: Harvard University Press, 1975), p. 2.

14. Cf. the opening lines of Virgil's second *Eclogue*, where Corydon is presented with a similar mixture of sympathy and amusement.

15. Hallett Smith, *Elizabethan Poetry* (Cambridge, Mass.: Harvard University Press, 1952), pp. 34-35.

16. *The Discovery of the Mind*, pp. 281-309.

17. *The Oxford Book of Sixteenth Century Verse*, ed. E. K. Chambers (Oxford: The Clarendon Press, 1932), p. 396.

18. *The Advancement of Learning*, II, xiii, in *The Works of Francis Bacon*, ed. R. L. Ellis, D. D. Heath, James Spedding (London: Longman and Co., 1860), 4:314-315.

19. *Literary Criticism*, ed. E. W. Tayler, p. 135.

20. *Apology*, p. 132.

21. *The Arte of English Poesie*, p. 38.

22. "Of Education," in *John Milton's Complete Poems*, ed. M. Hughes, p. 631; the second reference is from "The Reason of Church Government," p. 669.

23. *The Advancement of Learning*, II, xiii, in *Works*, 4: 315-316.

24. *The Arte of English Poesie*, p. 19.

25. *Apology*, p. 101.

26. *Ibid.*, p. 103.

27. In his Argument to Dryden's translation in *The Poetical Works of Dryden*, ed. G. R. Noyes (Boston: Houghton Mifflin, 1909) p. 431.

28. See E. W. Leach, pp. 235-36; also Zeph Steward, "The Song of Silenus," *Harvard Studies in Classical Philology* 64 (1959): 183-199.

29. *Works*, ed. Hebel, 2: 548.

30. Joan Grundy, *The Spenserian Poets* (London: Edward Arnold, 1969), p.74; H. E. Cory, "The Golden Age of the Spenserian Pastoral," *PMLA* 25 (1910): 241-267, surveys the work of these poets and notes their frequent echoes of "October."

## Chapter 2

1. See, for example, *Variorum*, vol. 7, pt 1, pp. 447-49.

2. For example, Peter Bayley, *Edmund Spenser: Prince of Poets* (London: Hutchinson University Library, 1971), pp. 79-84, makes a spirited defense of this neglected poem.

3. Samuel Johnson, *The Rambler,* ed. W. J. Bate and A. B. Strauss; *The Yale Edition of the Works of Samuel Johnson*, Vol. 3. (New Haven and London: Yale University Press, 1969), 1: 203; C. S. Lewis, *English Literature in the Sixteenth Century Excluding Drama* (New York and Oxford: Oxford University Press, 1954), p. 363.

4. Although my own interpretation will become clear in the discussion, this view has become orthodox among recent critics of the *Calender*. See, for example, Hallett Smith, *Elizabethan Poetry* (Cambridge, Mass.: Harvard University Press, 1952), p. 36. Also, A. C. Hamilton, "The Argument of Spenser's *Shepheardes Calender*," *ELH* 23 (1956): 171-182, argues that the poem's major theme is the poet's finding of himself; R. A. Durr, "Spenser's Calendar of Christian Time," *ELH* 24 (1957): 269-295, sees Colin's role as poet, lover, and priest as mutually inclusive; Isabel G. MacCaffrey, "Allegory and Pastoral in *The Shepheardes Calender*," *ELH* 36 (1969): 88-109, discusses the role of poetry as both a source of immortality and limited form of nonliteral action; Patrick Cullen, *Spenser, Marvell, and Renaissance Pastoral* (Cambridge, Mass.: Harvard University Press, 1970), pp. 76-98, argues that Colin, "however gifted in the order of poetry, cannot order his own life" (p. 81), that his "participation in romantic love becomes an excessive participation in the merely natural" (p. 78).

5. *Variorum*, Vol. 7, pt. 1, pp. 371-372, assesses Spenser's neoplatonic background with regard to the *Calender*.

6. Robert Ellrodt, *Neoplatonism in the Poetry of Spenser* (Geneva: Libraire E. Droz, 1960), p. 32.

7. *The Book of the Courtier*, trans. Thomas Hoby (London: Everyman's Library, 1928), p. 317. See also Sears Jayne, "Ficino and the Platonism of the English Renaissance," *Comparative Literature* 4 (1952): 214-238.

8. *The Book of the Courtier*, p. 319.

9. See Robert J. Clements, "The Cult of the Poet in Renaissance Emblem Literature," *PMLA* 59 (1944): 672-85, for a discussion linking poets to swans.

10. *The Book of the Courtier*, p. 318.

11. The pattern is easily observed in "May" in the debate between the worldly Palinode and the other-worldly Piers on the nature of the priesthood. The former urges freedom and an end of restriction (e.g., 71-72) while the latter argues for restraint (39-42). In the end Piers, whose tale of the fox and the kid describes the dangers of Palinode's view, carries the day. Cf. Patrick Cullen, pp. 29-76, who argues convincingly for the equilibrium of viewpoints in the moral debates. I am not challenging his valuable observations; but I suggest that Spenser is always keenly aware of the dangers of unrestrained freedom, with the result that the moral eclogues consistently emphasize the necessity of "restraint" and caution in human affairs.

12. It is not irrelevant perhaps to recall that the Italian word for "room" is *stanza*. Donne in "The Canonization" plays on a similar etymology when he rhapsodizes, "We'll build in sonnets pretty rooms."

13. For a good account of Orpheus's role in the *Calender* see Thomas H. Cain, "Spenser and the Renaissance Orpheus," *UTQ* 41 (1971): 24-47. It is worth remembering in this context that the mother of Orpheus is Calliope.

14. R. A. Durr sees Colin's role in "Aprill" as that of a priest as well as a poet, drawing men's souls to venerate the monarch. My own reading of the poem puts less stock in Colin's priestly function and more emphasis on his theatrical tone.

15. Patrick Cullen, pp. 112-119, has an ingenious, but not altogether convincing, reading of "Aprill" as an "allegory of the transforming power of Song" (p. 118) with Elisa as an ideal symbol of Astraea returning to preside over a new golden age of poetry. Thomas H. Cain, "The Strategy of Praise in Spenser's 'Aprill,'" *SEL* 8 (1968): 45-58, provides an expert reading of the hymn as a traditional encomium whose balanced structure reflects Colin's potentiality as a poet. The first half of the hymn shows Colin as "maker," the second half as visionary or seer. The hymn, Cain argues, is "Spenser's study of what a poet can do." (p. 58).

16. "Aprill," of course, is Hobbinol's recreation of Colin's hymn, as is the sestina in "August." Neither "Januarye," "December," nor "June" is performed by Colin for the benefit of an audience.

17. *Ovid's Metamorphoses: The Arthur Golding Translation, 1567*, ed. John Frederick Nims (New York: Macmillan, 1965), pp. 250-51 (10: 56-60).

18. For a compact treatment of this complex myth, see D. P. Walker, "Orpheus the Theologian and Renaissance Platonists," *Journal of the Warburg and Courtwald Institutes* 16 (1953): 102-120.

19. E. R. Curtius, *European Literature and the Latin Middle Ages*, trans. W. R. Trask (New York: Pantheon Books, 1953), pp. 83-85, outlines the "affected modesty" topos.

20. *Variorum*, vol. 7, pt. 1, p. 453, provides as complete a listing as possible of the identification of the various allegorical personages.

21. In addition to D. P. Walker, see William Nelson, *The Poetry of Edmund Spenser* (New York: Columbia University Press, 1963), pp. 100-115, who with some justness discusses this passage in connection with *The Fowre Hymnes.* Sam Meyer, *An Interpretation of Edmund Spenser's "Colin Clout"* (South Bend: Notre Dame University Press, 1969), although he resists discussing the roles of either Orpheus or neoplatonism in the poem, nonetheless makes many valuable remarks on this section of the poem, especially pp. 189-203.

## Chapter 3

1. *John Milton: English Poems, Comus, 1645* (Menston, England: The Scolar Press Limited, 1968), p. a5.

2. See Herbert E. Cory, *Spenser, the School of the Fletchers, and Milton* (Berkeley and Los Angeles: University of California Press, 1912).

3. Joan Grundy, *The Spenserian Poets* (London: Edward Arnold, 1969), pp. 204-17, concludes that Milton's earliest verse shows more signs of the influence of Spenser's "followers" than it does of Spenser.

4. *Poems of Mr. John Milton*, ed. Cleanth Brooks and John Edward Hardy (New York: Harcourt Brace, 1951), p. 246.

5. Louis Martz, "The Rising Poet, 1645," in *The Lyric and Dramatic Milton*, ed. Joseph Summers (New York: Columbia University Press, 1965), pp. 3-33.

6. *Poems of Mr. John Milton*, Brooks and Hardy, ed., pp. 263-268, makes a number of useful remarks about Milton and pastoral.

7. The frontispiece to Milton's volume is reporoduced in *The Lyric and Dramatic Milton*, ed. Joseph Summers, p. 6. Spenser's engraving is reproduced more frequently; for example, in *Spenser: Poetical Works*, ed. J. C. Smith and E. de Selincourt (London: Oxford University Press, 1912), p. 421.

8. *John Milton: Complete Poems,* ed. M. Hughes, p. 671.

9. William Haller, *The Rise of Puritanism* (New York: Columbia University Press, 1928), p. 306.

10. *John Milton: Complete Poems*, ed. M. Hughes, p. 669. For excellent discussions of Milton's vocational development, see A. S. P. Woodhouse, *The Heavenly Muse* (Toronto and Buffalo: University of Toronto Press, 1972), pp. 2-54; and John Spencer Hill, "Poet-Priest: Vocational Tension in Milton's Early Development," *Milton Studies* 8 (1975): 41-69.

11. See John R. Knott, Jr., *Milton's Pastoral Vision* (Chicago and London: University of Chicago Press, 1971), p. 53.

12. A. S. P. Woodhouse, *The Heavenly Muse*, p. 5, summarizes his famous account of Milton's "frame of reference" with regard to the order of nature and the order of grace. The design which I am unfolding has clear affinities with his classic description of the Renaissance imagination.

13. Anne Ferry, *Milton's Epic Voice: The Narrator in Paradise Lost* (Cambridge, Mass.: Harvard University Press, 1963), provides the most thorough treatment of Milton's creation of the narrative voice as a means to determine our response to his epic.

14. Kenneth R. R. Gros Louis, "The Triumph and Death of Orpheus in the English Renaissance," *SEL* 9 (1969): 63-80, makes a similar point. See also Caroline W.

Mayerson, "The Orpheus Image in *Lycidas*," *PMLA* 64 (1949): 189-207.

15. John Hollander, *The Untuning of the Sky* (Princeton: Princeton University Press, 1961), p. 170.

16. *Biographia Literaria*, ed. J. Shawcross (Oxford: Oxford University Press, 1907), 2:20.

17. In addition to John Hollander, see also G. L. Finney, *Musical Backgrounds for English Literature: 1580-1650 (New Brunswick: Rutgers University Press, 1962); Winifred Maynard, "Milton and Music" in John Milton: Introductions*, ed. John Broadbent (Cambridge: Cambridge University Press, 1973), pp. 226-257; S. K. Heninger, Jr., *Touches of Sweet Harmony: Pythagorean Cosmology and Renaissance Poetics* (San Marino: Huntington Library, 1974).

18. See A. S. P. Woodhouse and Douglas Bush, eds. *A Variorum Commentary on the Poems of John Milton* (London: Routledge and Kegan Paul, 1972), 2, pt. 1, pp. 34-38, for an assessment of Virgil's poem as Milton's model.

19. Lowry Nelson, Jr., *Baroque Lyric Poetry* (New Haven: Yale University Press, 1961), p. 51

20. Rosemond Tuve, *Images and Themes in Five Poems by Milton* (Cambridge, Mass.: Harvard University Press, 1957), pp. 42-43. See also Philip Rollinson, "Milton's Nativity Poem and the Decorum of Genre," *Milton Studies* 7 (1975): 165-188, for a thorough discussion of the poem's antecedents as a literary hymn.

21. Arthur Barker, "The Pattern of Milton's *Nativity Ode*," *UTQ* 10 (1941): 167-181.

22. Patrick Cullen, "Imitation and Metamorphosis: The Golden-Age Eclogue in Spenser, Milton, and Marvell," *PMLA* 84: 1559-1570.

23. R. Tuve, *Images and Themes*, p. 55.

24. For example, R. Tuve, *Images and Themes*, pp. 37-72 passim; also Laurence Stapleton, "Milton and the New Music," *UTQ* 13 (1953-54): 217-226, reprinted in *Milton: Modern Essays in Criticism* ed. Arthur Barker (New York: Oxford University Press, 1965), pp. 31-42.

25. Cf. R. Tuve, *Images and Themes*, pp. 57-58, who makes no sharp distinction between Milton's use of music and light imagery.

26. See Philip Rollinson, "Milton's Nativity Poem," 179-181, for other suggestions about the function of this section of the poem.

27. Lawrence W. Hyman, "Christ's Nativity and the Pagan Deities," *Milton Studies* 2 (1970): 103-112, deals with Milton's treatment of the "sense of loss we feel at the disappearance of the pagan gods" (p. 103).

28. For the classic discussion of the affected modesty *topos*, see Ernst Curtius, *European Literature and the Latin Middle Ages* trans. Willard R. Trask (New York: Pantheon Books, 1953), pp. 83-85.

29. For example, *Eclogue* 6, 1-12.

30. William Empson in a review of Cleanth Brooks's *The Well-Wrought Urn, Sewanee Review* 55 (1947): 691.

31. David M. Miller, "From Delusion to Illumination: A Larger Structure for *L'Allegro - Il Penseroso,*" *PMLA* 86 (1971): 32-39; also sees the poems suggesting a vertical structure as we pass from the first to the second. He confirms Don Cameron Allen, *The Harmonious Vision* (Baltimore: The Johns Hopkins Press, 1954), pp. 3-23.

# 212    SPENSER, MILTON, AND RENAISSANCE PASTORAL

32. The first opinion is that of E. M. W. Tillyard, *The Miltonic Setting* (London: Chatto and Windus, 1951), pp. 18-19; the second of Rosemond Tuve, *Images and Themes*, p. 24.

33. See, for example, *Poetry of John Milton* , ed Brooks and Hardy, pp. 135-136.

34. Nan C. Carpenter, "The Place of Music in *L'Allegro* and *Il Penseroso,*" *UTQ* 22 (1953): 354-367.

35. David M. Miller, "From Delusion to Illumination," pp. 36-37.

36. Kvester Svendsen, *The Explicator* 8 (1950), item 49.

37. Tillyard, *The Miltonic Setting,* pp. 18-19.

38. Maren-Sophie Røstvig, *The Happy Man: Studies in the Metamorphosis of a Classical Ideal* (Oslo: Akademisk forlag, 1954).

39. *John Milton: Complete Poems,* ed. M. Hughes, p. 625.

40. David M. Miller, "From Delusion to Illumination," 36-37.

41. Nan C. Carpenter, "The Place of Music," 366.

## Chapter 4

1. See, for example, G. S. Fraser, "Approaches to Lycidas," in *The Living Milton*, ed. Frank Kermode (London: Methuen, 1960), pp. 32-54; or Roberts W. French, "Voice and Structure in *Lycidas,*" TSLL  12 (1970): 15-24.

2. George Norlin, "The Conventions of the Pastoral Elegy," *American Journal of Philology* 32 (1911): 294-312, lists the following conventions of the form: (1) the guise of the herdsman moving amid rustic scenes; (2) a dramatic introduction and conclusion to the elegy proper; (3) a refrain; (4) the appeal to nature to mourn or the representation of nature as sharing in the universal sorrow; (5) the complaint to the nymphs and satyrs for their absence at the time of the death; (6) the trooping of divinities and friends to the grave of the corpse; (7) the command to deck the bier or grave with flowers; (8) the expression of bitter resentment at the fate which slits the thin-spun life; and (9) the realization that the dead is not really dead but lives on in another world. *The Pastoral Elegy: An Anthology*, ed. T. P.  Harrison and J. J. Leon (Austin: University of Texas Press, 1939), provides examples of the form and excellent notes and commentary.

3. "Notes on Convention," in *Perspectives of Criticism*, ed. Harry Levin, Harvard Studies in Comparative Literature, no. 20 (Cambridge, Mass: Harvard University Press, 1949), p. 77.

4. Northrop Frye, *Anatomy of Criticism: Four Essays* (Princeton: Princeton University Press, 1957), p. 105. Frye's discussion of convention is developed in his essay "Symbol as Archetype," pp. 95-115. Also, Ellen Zetzel Lambert, *Placing Sorrow: A Study Of the Pastoral Elegy Convention from Theocritus to Milton* (Chapel Hill: University of North Carolina Press, 1976), pp.xxi-xxxi, considers how the pastoral elegist's association of man and nature may derive from earlier funeral laments and vegetation rites.

5. *Anatomy of Criticism*, p. 107.

6. Renato Poggioli, *The Oaten Flute*, p. 65. Although I frequently disagree with Poggioli, his chapter "The Funeral Elegy," pp. 64-82, is the most acute and challenging treatment of the subject to date.

7. *The Harmonious Vision* (Baltimore: The Johns Hopkins Press, 1954), p. 63.

8. See *Ovid's Metamorphoses: The Arthur Golding Translation, 1567,* ed. John F. Nims (New York: Macmillan, 1965), pp. 367 (11. 1-88). For various accounts of the Orpheus legend that bear on pastoral, see Caroline W. Mayerson, "The Orpheus Image in *Lycidas*," *PMLA* 64 (1949): 189-207; William Berg, *Early Virgil* (London: Methuen, 1974), pp. 254-255; H. J. Rose, *A Handbook of Greek Mythology* (London: Macmillan, 1928), pp. 254-255; *The Pastoral Elegy: An Anthology,* Harrison and Leon, eds., pp. 1-3.

9. H. J. Rose, *Handbook,* pp. 124-125.

10. W. P. Mustard, "Later Echoes of the Greek Bucolic Poets," *American Journal of Philology* 30 (1911): 294-312, provides a compendium of sources for the Renaissance pastoral elegy; also James Holly Hanford, "The Pastoral Elegy and Milton's *Lycidas*," *PMLA* 25 (1910): 403-447, reprinted in Hanford's *John Milton: Poet and Humanist* (Cleveland: Western Reserve University Press, 1966), pp. 126-160, virtually exhausts the resources of the tradition in search of Milton's "indebtedness."

11. Andrew Lang, *Theocritus, Bion, and Moschus* (London: Macmillan, 1924), p. 171.

12. Poggioli, *The Oaten Flute,* p. 66.

13. *Greek Pastoral Poetry,* trans. Anthony Holden (London: Penguin Books, 1974), pp. 167-170. All translations of Moschus and Bion are from this edition.

14. Hanford, *John Milton,* p. 135.

15. Poggioli, *The Oaten Flute,* p. 70.

16. William Berg, *Early Virgil,* p. 124, discusses the role of Daphnis as a follower of Orpheus; see also Poggioli, p. 74.

17. See Michael C.J. Putnam, *Virgil's Pastoral Art* (Princeton: Princeton University Press, 1970), pp. 166-194, for an interesting discussion of this aspect of the eclogue. Putnam's book is a valuable study of the *Eclogues* from which all readers of Virgil in recent years have profited.

18. Putnam, *Virgil's Pastoral Art,* pp. 387-90, bases his discussion of the tenth *Eclogue* on its being Virgil's preparation to soar to the heights of epic.

19. Bruno Snell, *The Discovery of the Mind,* trans. T. G. Rosenmeyer (Cambridge, Mass: Harvard University Press, 1953), pp. 295-299.

20. Harrison's notes give a good picture of how often later poets relied on Virgil in shaping their pastoral elegies.

21. "Vergil and Spenser," *University of California Publications in English* 2, no. 3 (1929): 265-308.

22. Cf. Patrick Cullen, *Spenser, Marvell, and Renaissance Pastoral,* p. 145, who observes that "Dido in fact becomes a personification of the death of nature in winter, just as Elisa was a personification of the rebirth in spring."

23. See *Variorum,* pp. 500-505, for divergent views.

24. A facsimile edition is published in *The English Experience* series, no. 187 (Amsterdam and New York: De Capo Press, 1969).

25. Cf. William Nelson, *The Poetry of Edmund Spenser* (New York: Columbia University Press, 1963), p. 70: "Spenser avoided the personal note in this poem in order to set it apart from the lamentations which it introduces." Mr. Nelson does

not elaborate on this peculiar statement.

26. Cited by T. G. Rosenmeyer, *The Green Cabinet*, p. 113.

27. T. P. Harrison, "The Latin Pastorals of Milton and Castiglione" *PMLA* 50 (1935): 480-93.

28. A fine summary of the criticism of the poem is to be found in Douglas Bush, *A Variorum Commentary on the Poems of John Milton*, vol. 1, *The Latin and Greek Poems* (London: Routledge and Kegan Paul, 1970), pp. 284-297. A. S. P. Woodhouse, *The Heavenly Muse*, ed. Hugh MacCallum (Toronto: University of Toronto Press, 1972), pp. 83-92.

29. E. M. W. Tillyard, *Milton* (London: Chatto and Windus, 1920), pp. 99-100.

30. *Atque deos atque vocat crudelia mater*, Mopsus relates; "his mother taxed the gods and stars with cruelty."

31. Ralph Condee, "The Structure of Milton's *Epitaphium Damonis*," *SP* 62 (1965): 577-594.

32. *A Variorum Commentary*, p. 289.

33. J. S. Lawry, " 'Eager Thought': Dialectic in *Lycidas*," *PMLA* 77 (1962): 27-32, reprinted in Arthur Barker, ed., *Milton: Modern Essays in Criticism* (New York: Oxford University Press, 1963), pp. 112-124, reads the poem "as in part a dialectical process" of thesis, antithesis, and synthesis, but his methods and conclusions differ considerably from my own.

34. "Five Types of *Lycidas*," in *Milton's "Lycidas": The Tradition and the Poem*, ed. C. A. Patrides (New York: Holt, Rinehart, 1961), p. 213.

35. See especially Wayne Shumaker, "Flowerets and Sounding Seas: A Study in the Affective Structure of *Lycidas*," in Patrides, ed., pp. 125-35.

36. Isabel G. MacCaffrey, "*Lycidas*: Poet in a Landscape," in *The Lyric and Dramatic Milton*, ed. J. H. Summers (New York and London: Columbia University Press, 1965), pp. 75-77, provides an eloquent discussion of this section of the poem and its importance to the vision of experience the speaker gradually perceives.

37. See Caroline Mayerson, "The Orpheus Image in *Lycidas*," for a comprehensive account of Milton's use of the myth.

38. "Five Types of *Lycidas*," ed. Patrides, pp. 226-27.

39. Rosemond Tuve, *Images and Themes*, p. 96; Lowry Nelson, Jr., *Baroque Lyric Poetry*, p. 147.

40. Douglas Bush and A. S. P. Woodhouse, *A Variorum Commentary*, vol. 2, part 2, pp. 723-24, provide sources for the Michael reference and sort out the critical divergences that surround it.

41. *Milton*, ed. William G. Madsen (New York: Modern Library, 1964), p. 13.

42. Roberts W. French, "Voice and Structure in *Lycidas*," *TSLL* 12 (1970): 15-24.

43. "*Lycidas*: Poet in a Landscape," ed. J. H. Summers, p. 87.

## Chapter 5

1. *Poetical Works*, p. 407.

2. *Spenser's World of Glass* (Berkeley and Los Angeles: University of California Press, 1966), p. 190, Williams's essay on book 6 is among the most lively readings of the poem in recent years.

3. For an extreme example of a "pessimistic" view, see Richard Neuse, "Book VI as Conclusion to *The Faerie Queene,*" *ELH* 35 (1968): 329-53.

4. Paul Alpers, *The Poetry of "The Faerie Queene"* (Princeton: Princeton University Press, 1967). See also Isabel MacCaffrey, *Spenser's Allegory: The Anatomy of Imagination* (Princeton: Princeton University Press, 1976), pp. 343-420.

5. J. C. Maxwell, "The Truancy of Calidore," in *That Soveraine Light,* ed. William R. Mueller and D. C. Allen (Baltimore: Johns Hopkins Press, 1952), p. 69.

6. Humphrey Tonkin, *Spenser's Courteous Pastoral: Book VI of "The Faerie Queene"* (Oxford: Oxford University Press, 1972), p. 29. Although I disagree with Tonkin on particular issues, I concur for the most part with his admirable and challenging analysis of book 6 as an exploration of the metaphors of poetry and courtesy.

7. Kathleen Williams, *Spenser's World of Glass,* p. 203.

8. For example, Humphrey Tonkin, *Spenser's Courteous Pastoral,* p. 314.

9. Both Williams, pp. 200f., and Tonkin, passim, discuss the flower image and its relevance as a pastoral metaphor throughout the book. Both place what I see as a rather monocular emphasis on the flower as an image principally of life and re-birth.

10. See William Nestrick's sensitive essay "The Virtuous Discipline of Gentlemen and Poets," *ELH* 29 (1962): 357-71.

11. See Paul Alpers, *The Poetry of "The Faerie Queene",* p. 22 ff.

12. *Biographia Literaria,* ed. J. Shawcross, 2:11.

13. Compare Virgil's prologue to Pollio in *Eclogue* 8:

> a te principium, tibi desinet. accipe iussis
> carmina coepta tuis atque hanc sine tempora circum
> inter victrices hederam tibi serpere laurus.

> [11.13]

> My first notes were inspired by you: for you my last will
> sound. Accept this poem, begun at your command, and let
> its ivy twine with the victor's laurels round your brow.

14. *Spenser's Courteous Pastoral,* p. 142.

15. See Donald Cheney, *Spenser's Image of Nature: Wild Man and Shepherd in "The Faerie Queene"* (New Haven: Yale University Press, 1966), p. 177.

16. 2. 2, 3, 4, 5, 7, 10, 11, 13, 16, 20, 22, 23, 24, 25, 31, 35, 39, 41, 42, 45.

17. Compare 8.32, where Serena makes a false "return":

> Through hils and dales, through bushes and through breres
> Long thus she fled, till that at last she thought
> Her selfe now past the perill of her feares.

18. Calidore also "in his mind her worthy deemed" (9. 11). His reaction to Pastorella, in other words, is not merely superficial. One of the things he must learn is to come to terms with the profounder meaning of her physical beauty.

19. See, for example, Donald Cheney, *Spenser's Image of Nature,* pp. 231-36.

20. See Harry Berger, Jr., "A Secret Discipline: *The Faerie Queene,* Book VI," in *Form and Convention in the Poetry of Edmund Spenser,* ed. William Nelson (New York and London: Columbia University Press, 1961), pp. 35-75.

## Conclusion

1. *Apology*, p. 110.
2. Ibid., p. 120.

# Works Cited

Rather than compiling here a bibliography of the extensive scholarship and criticism surrounding Spenser, Milton, and pastoral, I have merely listed those books and articles cited in the foregoing notes pertaining most specifically to this study. I have not included any editions of either poet, nor have I listed the works of their contemporaries and predecessors.

Allen, Don Cameron. *The Harmonious Vision: Studies in Milton's Poetry*. Baltimore: The Johns Hopkins Press, 1954.

Alpers, Paul J. *The Poetry of "The Faerie Queene."* Princeton: Princeton University Press, 1967.

Barker, Arthur. "The Pattern of Milton's *Nativity Ode.*" *UTQ* 10 (1941): 167-81.

Bayley, Peter. *Edmund Spenser: Prince of Poets*. London: Hutchinson Library, 1971.

Berg, William. *Early Virgil*. London: Athlone Press, 1974.

Berger, Harry. "The Renaissance Imagination: Second World and Green World." *The Centennial Review* 9 (1965): 36-78.

———. "A Secret Discipline: *The Faerie Queene*, Book VI." In *Form and Convention in the Poetry of Edmund Spenser,* edited by William Nelson. New York: Columbia University Press, 1961.

Brooks, Cleanth, and Hardy, John Edward, eds. *Poems of Mr. John Milton*. New York: Harcourt Brace, 1951.

Bush, Douglas, and Woodhouse, A. S. P. *A Variorum Commentary on the Poems of John Milton*, vol. 2, pt. 1: *The Minor English Poems*, London: Routledge and Kegan Paul, 1972.

Cain, Thomas H. "Spenser and the Renaissance Orpheus." *UTQ* 41 (1971): 24-47.

————. "The Strategy of Praise in Spenser's 'April,'" *SEL* 8 (1968): 45-58.

Carpenter, Nan C. "The Place of Music in *L'Allegro* and *Il Penseroso.*" *UTQ* 22 (1953): 354-67.

Cheney, Donald. *Spenser's Image of Nature: Wild Man and Shepherd in "The Faerie Queene."* New Haven: Yale University Press, 1966.

Clements, Robert J. "The Cult of the Poet in Renaissance Emblem Literature." *PMLA* 59 (1944): 683-84.

Coleridge, Samuel Taylor. *Biographia Literaria.* Ed. by J. Shawcross. 2 vols. Oxford: Oxford University Press, 1907.

Condee, Ralph. "The Structure of Milton's *Epitaphium Damonis.*" *SP* 62 (1965): 577-94.

Cory, H. E. "The Golden Age of Spenserian Pastoral." *PMLA* 25 (1910): 241-67.

Cullen, Patrick. "Imitation and Metamorphosis: The Golden-Age Eclogue in Spenser, Milton, and Marvell." *PMLA* 84 (1969):

————. *Spenser, the School of the Fletchers, and Milton.* Berkeley and Los Angeles: University of California Press, 1912.

————. *The Infernal Triad: The Flesh, the World, and the Devil in Spenser and Milton.* Princeton: Princeton University Press, 1974.

————. *Spenser, Marvell, and Renaissance Pastoral.* Cambridge, Mass.: Harvard University Press, 1970.

Curtius, Ernst. *European Literature and the Latin Middle Ages.* Translated by W. R. Trask. New York: Pantheon Books, 1953.

Daiches, David. *Critical Approaches to Literature.* Englewood Cliffs: Prentice-Hall, 1956.

Durr, R. A. "Spenser's Calendar of Christian Time." *ELH* 24 (1957): 269-95.

Ellrodt, Robert. *Neoplatonism in the Poetry of Edmund Spenser.* Geneva: Libraire E. Droz, 1960.

Ferry, Anne D. *Milton's Epic Voice: The Narrator in "Paradise Lost."* Cambridge, Mass.: Harvard University Press, 1963.

Finney, G. L. *Musical Backgrounds for English Literature: 1580-1650.* New Brunswick: Rutgers University Press, 1962.

Fraser, G. S. "Approaches to Lycidas." *The Living Milton: Essays by Various Hands.* Edited by Frank Kermode. London: Routledge and Paul, 1960.

French, Roberts W. "Voice and Structure in Lycidas." *TSLL* 12 (1970): 15-24.

Frye, Northrop. *Anatomy of Criticism: Four Essays.* Princeton: Princeton University Press, 1957.

Giamatti, A. Bartlett. *The Earthly Paradise and the Renaissance Epic.* Princeton: Princeton University Press, 1966.

Greene, Thomas M. *The Descent From Heaven: A Study in Epic Continuity.* New Haven: Yale University Press, 1963.

Greenlaw, Edwin. "A Better Teacher Than Aquinas." *SP* 14 (1917): 196-217.

———. "Spenser's Influence on Paradise Lost." *SP* 17 (1920): 320-59.

Gros Louis, Kenneth R. R. "The Triumph and Death of Orpheus in the English Renaissance." *SEL* 9 (1969): 63-80.

Grundy, Joan. The Spenserian Poets: *A Study in Elizabethan and Jacobean Poetry.* London: Edward Arnold, 1969.

Haller, William. *The Rise of Puritanism.* New York: Columbia University Press, 1938.

Hamilton, A. C. "The Argument of Spenser's *Shepheardes Calender.*" *ELH* 23 (1956): 171-82.

Hanford, James Holly. *A Milton Handbook.* 4th ed. New York: Appleton, 1974.

Harrison, Thomas P. "The Latin Pastorals of Milton and Castiglione." *PMLA* 50 (1935): 480-93.

Harrison, Thomas P. and Leon, H. J., eds. *The Pastoral Elegy: An Anthology.* Austin: University of Texas Press, 1939.

Heninger, S. K., Jr. *Touches of Sweet Harmony: Pythogorean Cosmology and Renaissance Poetics.* San Marino: Huntington Library, 1974.

Hieatt, A. Kent. *Chaucer, Spenser, Milton: Mythopoeic Continuities and Transformations.* Montreal: McGill-Queens University Press, 1975.

Hill, John Spencer. "Poet-Priest: Vocational Tension in Milton's Early Development." *Milton Studies* 8 (1975): 41-69.

Hollander, John. *The Untuning of the Sky: Ideas of Music in Eng-*

*lish Poetry, 1500-1700.* Princeton: Princeton University Press, 1961.

Hughes, Merrit Y. "Vergil and Spenser." *University of California Publications in English*, Vol 2, No. 3 (1929): 263-428.

Hyman, Lawrence. "Christ's Nativity and the Pagan Deities." *Milton Studies* 2 (1970): 103-112.

Jayne, Sears. "Ficino and the Platonism of the English Renaissance." *Comparative Literature* 4 (1952): 214-38.

Kermode, Frank, ed. *English Pastoral Poetry: From the Beginnings to Marvell.* New York: The Norton Library, 1972.

Knott, John R. *Milton's Pastoral Vision: An Approach to "Paradise Lost."* Chicago and London: University of Chicago Press, 1971.

Lambert, Ellen Zetzel. *Placing Sorrow: A Study of the Pastoral Elegy Convention from Theocritus to Milton.* Chapel Hill: University of North Carolina Press, 1976.

Lang, Andrew. *Theocritus, Bion, and Moschus.* London: MacMillan, 1924.

Lawry, Jon S. " 'Eager Thought': Dialectic in *Lycidas*." PMLA 77 (1962): 27-32.

Leach, Elinor Winsor. *Virgil's "Eclogues": Landscapes of Experience.* Ithaca and London: Cornell University Press, 1974.

Levin, Harry. *The Myth of the Golden Age in the Renaissance.* Bloomington and London: University of Indiana Press, 1969.

———. "Notes on Convention" In *Perspectives of Criticism*, edited by Harry Levin. Harvard Studies in Comparative Literature, No. 20. Cambridge, Mass.: Harvard University Press, 1949.

Lewis, C. S. *The Allegory of Love: A Study in Medieval Tradition.* Oxford: Oxford University Press, 1936.

———. *English Literature in the Sixteenth Century Excluding Drama.* New York and Oxford: Oxford University Press, 1954.

MacCaffrey, Isabel. "Allegory and Pastoral in *The Shepheardes Calender*." *ELH* 36 (1969): 88-109.

———. "Lycidas: Poet in A Landscape." In *The Lyric and Dramatic Milton*, edited by Joseph Summers. New York: Columbia University Press, 1965.

————. *Spenser's Allegory: The Anatomy of Imagination.* Princeton: Princeton University Press, 1976.

Martz, Louis. "The Rising Poet, 1645." In *The Lyric and Dramatic Milton*, edited by Joseph Summers. New York: Columbia University Press, 1965.

Maxwell, J. C. "The Truancy of Calidore." In *That Soveraine Light*, edited by W. R. Mueller and D. C. Allen. Baltimore: The Johns Hopkins Press, 1952.

Mayerson, Caroline W. "The Orpheus Image in *Lycidas*." *PMLA* 64 (1949): 189-207.

Maynard, Winifred. "Milton and Music." In *John Milton: Introductions*, edited by John Broadbent. Cambridge: Cambridge University Press, 1973.

Meyer, Sam. *An Interpretation of Edmund Spenser's "Colin Clout."* South Bend: Notre Dame University Press, 1969.

Miller, David. "From Delusion to Illumination: A Larger Structure for *L'Allegro-Il Penseroso*." *PMLA* 86 (1971): 32-39.

Mustard, W. P. "Later Echoes of the Greek Bucolic Poets." *American Journal of Philology* 30 (1911): 245-83.

Nelson, Lowry, Jr. *Baroque Lyric Poetry.* New Haven: Yale University Press, 1961.

Nelson, William. *The Poetry of Edmund Spenser.* New York: Columbia University Press, 1963.

Nestrick, William. "The Virtuous Discipline of Gentlemen and Poets." *ELH* 29 (1962): 357-71.

Neuse, Richard. "Book VI as Conclusion to *The Faerie Queene*." *ELH* 35 (1968): 329-53.

Norlin, George. "The Conventions of the Pastoral Elegy." *American Journal of Philology,* 32 (1911): 294-312.

Patrides, C. A., ed. *Milton's "Lycidas": The Tradition and the Poem.* New York: Holt, Rinehart and Winston, 1961.

Poggioli, Renato. *The Oaten Flute: Essays on Pastoral Poetry and the Pastoral Ideal.* Cambridge, Mass.: Harvard University Press, 1975.

Putnam, Michael, C. J. *Virgil's Pastoral Art: Studies in the "Eclogues."* Princeton: Princeton University Press, 1970.

Rollinson, Philip. "Milton's Nativity Poem and the Decorum of

Genre." *Milton Studies* 7 (1975): 165-88.

Rose, H. J. *A Handbook of Greek Mythology.* London: MacMillan, 1928.

Rosenmeyer, Thomas G. *The Green Cabinet: Theocritus and the European Pastoral Lyric.* Berkeley and Los Angeles: University of California Press, 1969.

Røstvig, Maren-Sophie. *The Happy Man: Studies in the Metamorphosis of an Ideal.* 2 vols. Oslo: Akademisk forlag, 1954.

Smith, Hallett. *Elizabethan Poetry.* Cambridge, Mass.: Harvard University Press, 1952.

Snell, Bruno. *The Discovery of the Mind: The Greek Origins of European Thought.* Translated by T. G. Rosenmeyer. Cambridge, Mass.: Harvard University Press, 1953.

Stapleton, Laurence. "Milton and the New Music." *UTQ* 40 (1953-54): 217-26.

Steward, Zeph. "The Song of Silenus." *Harvard Studies in Classical Philology* 64 (1959): 183-99.

Svendsen, Kvester. *The Explicator* 8 (1950), item 49.

Tayler, Edward W. *Nature and Art in Renaissance Literature.* New York: Columbia University Press, 1961.

Tillyard, E. M. W. *Milton.* London: Chatto and Windus, 1930.

————. *The Miltonic Setting.* London: Chatto and Windus, 1951.

Tonkin, Humphrey. *Spenser's Courteous Pastoral: Book VI of "The Faerie Queene."* Oxford: Oxford University Press, 1972.

Tuve, Rosemond. *Images and Themes in Five Poems by Milton.* Cambridge, Mass.: Harvard University Press, 1957.

Walker, D. P. "Orpheus the Theologian and Renaissance Platonists." *Journal of the Warburg and Courtwald Institutes* 16 (1953): 102-20.

Williams, Kathleen. "Milton, Greatest Spenserian." In *Milton and the Line of Vision*, edited by Joseph A. Wittreich, Jr. Madison: University of Wisconsin Press, 1975.

' ————. *Spenser's World of Glass: A Reading of "The Faerie Queene."* Berkeley and Los Angeles: University of California Press, 1966.

Woodhouse, A. S. P. *The Heavenly Muse: A Preface to Milton.* Edited by Hugh MacCallum. Toronto: University of Toronto Press, 1972.

# Index